If This Marriage Was Made In Heaven, Why Am I Going Through Hell?

*A Biblical Model for Marriage:
Restoring Its Virtue and Value*

If This Marriage Was Made In Heaven, Why Am I Going Through Hell?

A Biblical Model for Marriage:
Restoring Its Virtue and Value

Karry D. Wesley

Packaged by WinePress Publishing, PO Box 428, Emumclaw, WA 98022. The views expressed or implied in this work do not necessarily reflect those of WinePress Publishing. Ultimate design, content, and editorial accuracy of this work are the responsibilities of the author(s).

Unless otherwise noted all scriptures are taken from the Holy Bible, New International Version, Copyright © 1973, 1978, 1984 by the International Bible Society. Used by permission of Zondervan Publishing House. The "NIV" and "New International Version" trademarks are registered in the United States Patent and Trademark Office by International Bible Society.

ISBN 1-57921-282-4
Library of Congress Catalog Card Number: 99-69936

Dedication

*This book is dedicated to my wife, Cheryl.
She is a God-sent companion whom I
love dearly.*

Contents

Introduction

When I was growing up, it wasn't uncommon to hear or read about couples celebrating their golden wedding anniversaries. Those couples reached that milestone for several reasons. First of all, they believed in the sacredness of marriage. They believed that the vows made before God should be honored by both partners. Also, they were able to reach the milestone by working together to make the marriage last. They did not bail out of the marriage when problems surfaced. They did whatever they thought was necessary to make the marriage work. Lastly, they were able to reach the milestone by focusing on the genuine love they had for each other. Love made the marriage last.

It is evident that the times have changed. Some married couples barely allow the ink to dry on the marriage license before filing for divorce. The statistics on marriage today show that the majority of the couples getting married will also get divorced. What happened to the sacredness of the institution? Why aren't we witnessing more marriages that last until "death do us part?" Is there anything that can be done to help those "united" in marriage to never become "untied?" Hopefully, the material in this book will be helpful.

If This Marriage Was Made In Heaven, Why Am I Going Through Hell?

The title of this book comes from an episode that I witnessed while counseling a Christian couple in the church where I serve as pastor. They met while serving in one of the ministries of the church. They had been married for over eight years before this episode occurred in my office. They have always been actively involved in the church and they really love the Lord. Everyone in the church knew that God brought them together. One day, while the husband sat in the car, the wife approached me with tears in her eyes. Once she entered the office, she looked at me and said, *Pastor, if this marriage was made in heaven, please tell me why I am going through hell?*

After hearing that question, I decided to write this book. As a matter of fact, the material in this book was used to help that couple through their problems. Five years later, they are still together. I wanted to offer the saints of God a biblically-based book to help them through those difficult moments that we all face in our marriages. The book gives a lot of common sense methods that will help couples have a loving and lasting relationship. It deals with everything from communication to sex.

The material in this book is designed to offer some biblical medicine to help mend and heal marriages that are on the verge of disaster. The book offers biblical ways to resolve the conflict and restore the passion. The material in this book will also be helpful for those who are considering marriage in the future. For too long, many couples have entered the institution of marriage without having any idea what God says about the institution that He established. The book also addresses what Christian men and women should look for in a God-sent mate. I advise men and women to read the book before the question is popped.

This book will also help engaged couples to start off on the right foot. I will be the first to admit that I was somewhat nervous after I became a husband. I really didn't know what to expect. I had a lot of questions and did not know who to ask. This book answers a lot of those questions. There are many couples that have the survival plan working just fine in their marriages. They are not on the verge of divorce and they are happy with each other. This book can help them to move from merely surviving in the marriage to a point of thriving in the marriage.

Chapter 1

Don't Just Leap into Marriage

> It is better to be living single than to be married to someone who is living as though he is single.
> —Pastor Samuel Morris

But seek ye first the kingdom of God, and his righteousness; and all these things shall be added unto you.
—Matthew 6:33 KJV

Before we deal specifically with the marriage covenant, I think it is necessary to talk about the stage before you get there. It is important for marriages in trouble to reach back to the past in order to deal with the present. The foundation that you build on will have an effect on your future stability. If the foundation of the marriage was established on something other than the Word of God, that is probably the reason for the present problems.

I must say something to the single person reading this book. There are many people who have developed an anti-marriage philosophy. Many fear marriage because of what they have seen happen in other marital relationships. They vow never to marry because of the pain they saw their mother or father witness in a "bad" marriage. If your foundation is solid, you don't have to worry about duplicating what existed in another marriage.

There are many that are single and looking forward to the day when they leap into holy matrimony. This expectation is a good thing. The Scripture supports this in Genesis 2:18 by saying, "It is not good for the man to be alone" (NIV). Unless you are "giftedly" single, you should anticipate marriage one day. However, there are some cautions that you should be aware of before you "jump the broom." These precautions can help you avoid a marriage destined for hell's pit.

Looking Before You Leap

If you don't look before you leap, you can end up traveling down the road of disaster, destruction, and, yes, even divorce. A large number of people end up like Jacob in the book of Genesis. Do you remember what happened to him? He worked seven years for Laban for the hand of his daughter Rachel. At the end of the seven-year period, Laban gave Jacob his daughter to marry. Jacob went in that night and consummated the marriage, only to awaken the next morning to discover that he had married Leah, the other daughter of Laban, rather than Rachel (Gen. 29:16–25). You can end up with a Leah or a Lee instead of your Rachel or Ricky, if you don't look before you leap.

When I say *look*, I am not just speaking about using your eyes to check out his or her physical features. There are those who thought outward appearances were sufficient, only to discover the next morning that they had married someone who had some nice physical features, but inwardly they looked like the Wicked Witch of the West. A car can have a good body, but if the engine is no good, it's a lemon. It is a good thing to remember that everything that looks good is not always good for you. The nephew of Abraham can testify to this truth.

One day, Lot approached his Uncle Abram after their herdsmen had been arguing over water and grazing rights for their cattle, and said that something needed to be done. Abram shared with his nephew that they should not fall out over the issue. Abram gave Lot an opportunity to select whatever portion of the land he wanted. Lot looked up and saw this beautiful land to the east and said, "I'll take that land over there." It looked great! It was Sodom and Gomorrah; and you know what eventually happened to that place (Gen. 13:5–13; 19:20).

Marriage is an important step to take in life. We must leave the matchmaking up to God. He knows who is just right for us. He knows who is compatible. I believe God will send the right mate, but there are some things He expects us to do in the process. We should be able to look and see someone who is godly, gifted, good, great, and gorgeous (in that order).

Living Before You Leap

It is so important for you to live before you leap. Before you get excited about this point, let me explain. When I say *live*, I am not speaking of "sowing your wild oats" before you get married. I am not saying that you should let your hair down before you marry. When I speak of living, I am speaking of what Jesus spoke of when He said, "I came that you might have life and have it more abundantly (John 10:10 KJV)." I am speaking of what Paul expressed in Phillipians 1: 21, when he said "For to me, to live is Christ and to die is gain," (Philippians 1:21 KJV).

How can you identify a God-sent mate if you are not living the life yourself? If there are no godly attributes visible in your life, how do you expect to attract someone who is godly? The life you live will determine if you find the person divinely designed for you. The path you travel will determine whether or not you will meet Mr. Right or Miss Right. If your life travels on the road of sin, you will meet someone, but it will not be the one God has prepared for you.

When you live for Christ, several things are happening in your life. First of all, you are *Single and Saved*. You have received the grace of God by faith. You have followed the prescription of Romans 10:9 that says, "If thou shall confess with thy mouth the Lord Jesus and shall believe in thine heart that God hath raised him from the dead, thou shalt be saved" (KJV).

Next, it means you are *Single and Sanctified*. You have separated your life from the ways of the world. You have decided not to "fulfil the lust of the flesh . . . (KJV)" You have decided to commit your life to God.

It also means you are *Single and Submissive*. You have decided to submit to the will of God for your life. You have decided to allow God to lead you in all that you do. You have decided to "submit yourself to God, resist the devil and he will flee from you (James 4:7 KJV)."

It means you are *Single and Satisfied*. You have learned to appreciate who you are, as well as, accept what you have as sufficient. You have "learned whatever state you are in to be contented (Philippians 4:11 KJV)."

Last, you are *Single and Selective*. You have decided to be selective in those with whom you have relations. You are committed to being "equally yoked" in all relationships. When you live independently of Christ, the opposite is probably true. You are *Single and Secular*. You follow the ways of the world, rather than the will of God. The world brings temporary pleasure into your life.

It could mean you are *Single and Scandalous*. There are really no rules followed except those that bring about personal satisfaction. You don't mind hurting people to get what you want. You will play with the emotions of people without a guilt-stricken conscience.

It could also mean you are *Single and Sensual*. You are carnal in nature. You will allow carnality to lead you to search for your mate in the club rather than the church.

Last, it could also mean you are *Single and Seductive*. Your dress code, walk, and body become a tool to lure him or her in. Your language is geared to produce lust rather than love.

Paul records in Romans 12:1 (KJV)

> I beseech you therefore, brethren, by the mercies of God, that ye present your bodies a living sacrifice, holy, acceptable unto God, which is your reasonable service. And be not conformed to this world: but be ye transformed by the renewing of your mind, that ye may prove what is that good, and acceptable, and perfect will of God.

Your way of living will determine whether or not the perfect or permissive will of God will be done in your life. If your life is one that delights in the Lord, "He will give you the desires of your heart" (Psalm 37:4 KJV). It is wise to live before you leap.

Listening Before You Leap

Don't leap without listening to the voice of God. Too often, we fail to ask God to speak to our hearts regarding the relationships we enter. We should ask God to reveal His will to us regarding him or her. When we pray for God's will to be revealed, we should listen to what He has to say to us. Too many ask Him to show them, and when

He does, they ignore the revelation. The problem is that our prayers are sometimes rendered with certain selfish attachments included. We expect God to reveal what we want rather than what is real or what it is that He wants for us.

When you ask God to reveal things about him or her, and all of a sudden the person begins to reveal his or her true character God is answering your prayer. When you suddenly witness abusive behavior, God is speaking. When you observe continuous lying and deceit, God is answering your prayer. God speaks to us by allowing us to see certain things. Listen to what God is saying.

Proverbs 1:24, 25 says, "Because I have called, and ye refused; I have stretched out my hand, and no man regarded. But you have set at naught all my counsel, and would none of my reproof" (KJV). Many listen to God, but due to their own desires, they convince themselves that God has some special plans to change him or her after they are married. There have been others that have been physically abused before marriage who thought the same way. They figured he would change after the vows were exchanged, only to discover that the abuse got worse. There have been those who thought her unfaithfulness would stop after marriage, only to discover that the marriage vows didn't mean anything to her.

When you seek God's voice, remember that He answers through His Word. His word says, "Ye shall know them by their fruit" (Matthew 7:16 KJV). When He speaks to us, we should listen to His voice without trying to bargain with Him. He knows what, as well as who, is best for us.

Laboring Before You Leap

One of the most impressive things about Jacob's desire to win the hand of Rachel was his willingness to work fourteen years for her. He was a hard worker. This is commendable in any man. If the spirit of laziness exists before marriage, watch out. The first part of Proverbs 12:11 says, "He that tilleth his land shall be satisfied with bread" (KJV). If he won't work, and shows no concern in looking for a job, he is not for you. If you have become a lending institution for him, and those loans have defaulted, leave him alone. Don't think he is going to have this sudden change in regard to the work ethic after you exchange vows.

First Timothy 5:8 says, "If anyone does not provide for his own, and especially for those of his own household, he has denied the faith, and is worse than an unbeliever" (KJV). God expects the husband to be a provider for the family. He must be someone who is willing to work in order to take care of his household. A marriage cannot survive on love alone. Love will not pay the rent. It can't be used at your local grocer. It can't put gas in the car. Love plus an income are required.

I am not suggesting that you check out his P.O.E. (place of employment) status to see if he is the one for you. I believe many men and women have missed their blessings by dismissing a person because the individual was not making the salary figure desired. Who knows what may be in store? If he or she is a hard worker with drive and ambition, you may be missing out on the best thing that could happen to you. I have heard many success stories from individuals who started off with very little, but due to ambition and drive, they now have excelled financially.

Learning Before You Leap

People have often asked me, "How long should an engagement last before marriage?" My response is, "You should make sure you know who you are marrying." None of us are so connected to God that we can actually tell if he or she is the one when he or she is first seen. How can you know he is the one if you don't even know him? How can you know she is the one if this is your first time meeting her? The answer to both questions is that you can't know if he or she is the one by only looking.

I remember as a freshman in college, a young lady approached me after chapel and said that she wanted to talk to me about something, and I said okay. As we walked toward the cafeteria, she said, "I want you to know that God told me you were the one."

"What did he tell you I was the one for?" I asked.

"He told me that you were going to be my husband." I told her, "I just finished talking to God in chapel. He talked to me but didn't mention your name." Obviously, God was talking about someone else. I wonder if she ever got married?

Compatibility in a marriage requires more than both of you liking anchovies on your pizza. It requires more than both of you working in the same field or liking the same kind of movies. You need to make sure that your personalities don't clash. The length of the courtship should be based on making sure he or she is someone you can spend the rest of your life with. This cannot be determined after one date.

Laughing Before You Leap

I had a young woman's father approach me years ago and say, "Pastor Wesley, after you met with my daughter and her fiancé a couple of times, they decided to call off the wedding. What happened?" I shared with him that I start off all of my counseling sessions telling the counselee that the only way the information that they share leaves my office is if they take it out. I told him that I could not divulge the information. I then asked him what was his deepest concern with the decision they had made not to get married. He said, "I think she is making a grave mistake. I think the young man is a good guy. I really enjoy sitting around talking to him. He likes working on cars like I do. We both like to bass fish." I gave one response to all of the things he mentioned by saying, "It is good to know the two of you have a good time together, but who was he marrying?"

The young lady and young man didn't have the same story for their relationship with each other. As a matter of fact, the story was just the opposite. You need to be happy with each other, because you are the ones getting married. Listen, if you cannot laugh and have a good time with him or her before marriage, what do you think is going to happen when you get married and see each other all the time?

You don't need anyone you don't like being around. If you dread being in his presence, you shouldn't marry him. If she causes you to get depressed rather than excited, you shouldn't marry her. If there is more fussing and fighting than fun and folly, you don't need to get married. If he or she makes your skin crawl rather than causes a tinkle to run down your spine, you probably shouldn't marry him or her.

Marriage should be a time filled with more happy days than sad days. If you can't get along now, why do you expect that to change? A good way to test this point is to examine how you feel about certain things. Do you miss him when he is gone, or is it a time of pleasure for you? Do you think positive thoughts about her when she is not around? Do you look forward to getting together, or do you wish something would come up so that the date can be canceled? Do you enjoy talking on the phone, or do you find yourself always wondering if someone else is on the other end because you can't think of anything to say to each other?

Make sure you enjoy each other now. Don't leap if there is not a great deal of joy in your present relationship.

— Chapter 2 —

The First Marriage

> Marriage is surely one of the most serene and sublime blessings God has bestowed on humanity.
> —William J. McRae

And the rib, which the Lord God had taken from man, made he a woman, and brought her unto the man.

—Gen. 2:22

The First Marriage

To get started with our lessons on marriage, let's go back to the very beginning when marriage was instituted. We can find a description of this first marriage in Genesis 2:18–24:

> Then the Lord God said, "It is not good for man to be alone: I will make him a helper suitable for him." And out of the ground the Lord God formed every beast of the field and every bird of the sky, and brought them unto the man to see what he would call them; and whatever the man called a living creature that was its name. And the man gave the names to all the cattle, and the birds of the sky, and to every beast of the field, but for Adam there was not found a helper suitable for him. So the Lord caused a deep sleep to fall upon the man, and

he slept; then He took one of his ribs, and closed up the flesh at that place. And the Lord God fashioned into a woman the rib which he had taken from the man, and brought her to man. And the man said, "This is bone of my bones, and flesh of my flesh; she shall be called Woman, because she was taken out of Man." For this cause a man shall leave his father and his mother, and shall cleave to his wife; and they shall become one flesh. (KJV)

If couples would spend time examining what took place in this passage, I believe many of the problems facing the institution of marriage today would be resolved. This account of the first marriage gives us a foundation to build upon. Let's take a closer look at the things that took place when the first marriage transpired.

The Problem Disclosed

It is interesting that there is only one "not good" listed in the entire creative process. It is found in these verses. It was God that said, "It is not good for man to be alone." It was God that recognized man's state of loneliness. It was God that recognized the need of man to have someone else made in his likeness to complete him.

Whenever we face a need in our lives, God is there to do something about it. God is capable of changing a not-good situation to a good situation. We should understand that the not-good portion of the creative process does not point to a mistake made by God. You can almost picture this scene with Adam. He notices that as God brings the different animals to him to be named, there is a companion for each. There is a male and a female. But he was all alone. It probably appeared to be an unfair world for Adam. From God's perspective, it did not point to an unfair world, but an unfinished work. It really points to some unfinished work that God was going to perform before He said, "It is finished." God was knowledgeable all along of this problem in man.

When you read the Genesis account, note that God sees the problem, and not Adam. No where in the creation story do you read about Adam's displeasure with anything. God saw a need to address the problem that Adam didn't even realize he had. God was willing to answer a question that hadn't even surfaced. God decided to resolve an issue that hadn't really become an issue.

What an awesome God we serve. He knows our needs even before we do. He is willing to address problems of which we are sometimes unaware. I used to hear my grandmother say something in her prayers that I didn't understand as a child. She would say, "Father, I thank You for bringing me through dangers seen and unseen." My grandmother explained to me later what she meant by that prayer. She explained by saying, "There are times when we see certain dangers in our lives and God will step in and make a way for us. There are other times when He will intercept the danger without us ever seeing it."

In Genesis 2:18, we read about God's disclosure of humanity's need. God is aware of what is missing in our lives. This is why the Word of God teaches us that "He knows our needs even before we ask him" (Matthew 6:8 KJV).

The Plan Determined

There is no problem too big for our God. He knew exactly what He was going to do to address the "unknown" problem facing Adam. Look at how God determined within Himself to deal with man's problem. He said, "I will make a helper, suitable for him." God recognized the problem and decided to do something about it. God decided He would make someone just right for Adam. He knew what Adam needed and decided to draft a plan to take care of that need. The plan called for producing a helper who was suitable for him. God knew that Adam needed someone to help him to manage, or to provide order for, his life. What he needed had to be suitable or complimentary to his nature. The rest of the animal kingdom could not fit the bill. God had a plan for someone just right to be designed for him. This plan would address the need of Adam.

Many read the account of God's plan to produce Eve as an afterthought of God. This can't be the case. God had intentions of producing a compatible creature for the prize of His creation from the beginning. The very physiological and psychological structures of humanity suggest this point. God didn't produce Adam and later produce a sex drive in him. This was a part of his physiological makeup from the beginning. It is probably true that the production of Eve made this physiological structure more apparent.

God had plans for addressing Adam's need. He knew what He was going to do to provide suitable companionship for Adam. This is true for all that are to marry. We should allow God to do the planning. He is more knowledgeable of our needs than we are. It is evident from the text that Adam knew something was missing, but he didn't know what was needed. We sometimes think we know, but remember, our Heavenly Father knows best. He knows what man or woman is suitable for all of us. We should allow God to plan for us because He knows who is best for us.

The Procedure Described

Next, look at the description given to us regarding the procedure used by God to prepare a mate for Adam. God became a divine anesthesiologist and placed Adam in a deep sleep. I would love to know what Adam was dreaming about as he slept. I wonder if God caused Adam to see a vision of loveliness in his dreams that he couldn't really explain after awakening from his slumber. I believe that God sometimes speaks and reveals through dreams. We can see this in the lives of biblical personalities like Joseph, Nebuchadnezzar, and others.

As Adam dreams and snoozes, God decides to take from Adam's body the substance needed to produce Eve. Why didn't He choose to produce Eve the same way He produced Adam? Could it be that Adam would appreciate something much more that came from him rather than anything else? The reason God chose this route is not revealed.

Someone has suggested that God chose to do this in order that Adam would recognize the importance of his gift. God chose to take a rib from the side to suggest to Adam that he had a helper to walk side by side with him in life. He chose a rib because of its closeness to the heart. He chose a rib to remind Adam that his companion was produced from his inner parts and not one of the animals he named.

There was a man looking at an X-ray of his chest and he exclaimed to his wife, "I didn't really accept that creation story about Eve. Do you see a rib missing from this X-ray?" The wife responded by saying, "Sometimes I wonder why God put men in charge. How do you expect that which is missing to be there in the first place?"

The Present Delivered

Let me use my imagination for a moment here. Adam awakens out of his sleep and probably thinks he had never slept like that before. He sits up and stretches. One of the animals comes over to where he is, and Adam starts petting the animal on the head.

He says to the cat, "I dreamed about another creature that looked sort of like me. She was different in certain areas but she had a lot of similar features. We were running through the garden and doing something similar to what I have seen you and tomcat doing." He stops talking to the cat and says, "Here I am talking to this cat as if it really understands me."

Then Adams hears God walking in the midst of the garden. He thinks to himself, *I'll tell God about this incredible dream I had. He will understand it.* He turns around, and there, standing with his Maker, is the same figure from his dream. The only difference is that he is not asleep now. God delivered Adam the best present ever.

Adam didn't find Eve one day while sitting by the brook. He didn't stumble upon Eve. The Bible tells us that God brought Eve to Adam. God actually gave away the first bride. God decided to personally deliver this gift to Adam. When you recognize a blessing that you have received from God, you will express gratitude, not only in word, but in action as well. God delivered this present (unwrapped) for Adam's enjoyment as well as Eve's.

Whenever God gives us something special, we should be careful how we treat His special gift. Marriage should be viewed as something special because it is a blessing from God. Since marriage is a blessing from God, we must be careful as to how we refer to it when we are talking about it. We should never speak of our blessings from God in a negative manner. Whenever you hear people using cutting language in describing their mates, they are actually showing a lack of appreciation for the blessing that God gave.

The Partnership Discovered

It was at this point, I believe, that Adam realized that God took care of a problem he had even before he knew about it. It was a dream come true for Adam. God had produced someone likened unto him so that he could have someone with whom to share. When God provided Eve for Adam, it was evident that Adam accepted what he was given as a partner and not a slave. He recognized that what he received was a part of him and no other creature. His response to the provision was, "This is bone of my bones . . ." His response implies that he understood that she was not made of any inferior substance. Nor was she made from any superior substance. She was made from the same substance of which he was made.

Adam not only knew that a part of him was used to produce Eve, he also knew that she was created with the same physiological attributes as himself. This is why he said, "This is . . . flesh of my flesh . . ."

Adam now had someone in his life that was able to bring about completion for him. As he touches her, he is able to see that she didn't feel like the rest of the animals in the garden. She was made out of something special. He noticed all of those similar physical features and was excited.

This understanding would evidently cause him to treat her as a partner and not a slave. God never intended for women to be treated as inferior people. They are made from the same substance. Neither did He intend for women to act as though they are superior. His desire is for us to look at one another as partners with a common bond. The common bond is that both the male and female were created in the *imago Dei* (the image of God).

The Parting Defined

God never intended for a couple to get married and move in with one or the other's parents. Marriage represents starting one's own household. In the Genesis passage, the text tells us what God expected for future marriages. The text records; "For this cause shall a man leave his father and his mother and cleave to his wife." In order for the marriage to work the way it was intended to work, there must be a parting from parents. The marriage cannot blossom as God intended without a detachment.

As parents, my wife and I have the responsibility of rearing our boys in the fear and admonition of the Lord. We must teach and train them according to the Word of God. We must provide shelter, support, and substance as they go through their developmental stages in life. There are certain rules and regulations that we set and expect for them to follow. There will come a point when our parental responsibility ends, and their responsibility begins.

The Permanence Declared

God never intended for people to be in one marital relationship today and out tomorrow. The statistics indicating that one out of two marriages end in divorce was never connected to the plan of God. It was God's intention for the husband and wife to be glued together for life. This is what the Genesis passage is dealing with when the word *cleave* is used.

God's plan included permanence. Couples shouldn't enter the institution of marriage saying, "I'll get a divorce if it doesn't work out," or, "I can give it a try, and if it is not for me, I will bail out." This is not in the will of God. God desires for couples to cleave, or stick together, for the long haul.

Chapter 3

The Role of the Husband

> Biblical leadership is clearly not a place of ease and advantage, but a calling to work, sacrifice, and service.
> —William Hendricks

Likewise, ye husbands, dwell with them according to knowledge, giving honor unto the wife, as unto the weaker vessel, and as being heirs together of the grace of life; that your prayers be not hindered.

—1 Pet. 3:7

The Role of the Husband

We are living in an age in which little emphasis is placed on roles in a marriage. There is little distinction placed on what the husband, as well as the wife, is to do in the marriage. Through the years, the design of roles in marriages has been lost to the extent that what we see now, I call "role-less marriages." As Christians, we should not de-emphasize roles, but properly define them according to the Scripture. Many see roles as confining. They view the concept of roles in marriage as a tool to promote some unfair or impartial act.

Since God is responsible for establishing the institution of marriage, it is important to operate within the boundaries set by Him. We cannot operate according to the world's view. We must get rid of the feminist mentality, as well as the macho man perspective, to rightly understand the institution of marriage. The Bible is very clear about how a marriage should be organized. The marriage will not work if we operate according to what we see on television or read about in some novel. We must allow the Bible to serve as the how-to book for our marriages.

It is difficult for those in the world to accept the format outlined by God, when operating their marriages. To them, it appears that God is chauvinistic and promotes dominance and oppression of women. When you look at the words used in describing the roles for husbands and wives, there appears to be an unfair imbalance. The Bible uses words like *head, protect,* and *provide* when speaking to husbands, and *helper, lover, obey,* and *submission* when speaking to wives. It really appears on the surface to be unfair, but this was not God's intention.

When you examine the meaning behind those passages in Scripture using this terminology, you will discover that it is not a "rank" issue but a "role" issue. It is not a "rule" issue but a "responsibility" issue. God has distinct roles and responsibilities given to cause the marriage to flow the way it should. Those words point to distinct roles determined by God for those who are married. The husband is responsible for a specific kind of leadership. The wife is responsible for a specific kind of support and nurture. It is all designed to be complementary, with both in the front seat of the car, but only one driving. It is also like the pilot and copilot in the cockpit of the 747 jet. In order to have a safe landing there are certain duties, just as important as the others, that both must perform.

The Husband as Leader

The role of the husband has been misunderstood down through the years. It was never designed to advocate the oppression of women. It has very little to do with "being the boss" in the relationship. As a matter of fact, in a biblical marriage, the husband's role revolves around the subject of leadership. This leadership is not a dictator style. That is what the world offers. Force and domination serve as its mode of operation. This style has caused many women to suffer hurt, hell, and humiliation. This is not the appropriate style of leadership.

Scriptures relating to marriage are more connected to a loving style of leadership. This style of leadership focuses on caring and serving rather than being served. It emphasizes support rather than superiority. It emphasizes task rather than title. This style follows a pattern set forth by Jesus in Luke 22:24–26. In the Luke passage, Jesus rebukes a leadership style that leads to abusive power. Look at what he says in Luke 22:25:

> And he said unto them, The kings of the Gentiles exercise lordship over them; and they that exercise authority upon them are called benefactors (KJV).

This dictator style is designed specifically for selfish gain. A benefactor is one who receives the benefits. The husband exercising this kind of leadership is concerned about himself only.

It is important to recognize that the emphasis should never be on dominance but duty. God simply gives an organizational arrangement that will cause the marriage to work the way it was designed to work. The responsibilities given are not designed to cause one to be considered more important than the other. God desires for the husband and wife to share. The husband was never called by God to be a dictator or a slave master. The wife is neglected and abused in this style of leadership. The husband operating from this style will do whatever it takes to make sure his needs are met and will totally ignore the needs of his wife and children.

Look at what Jesus says next in Luke 22:26: *"But you shall not be so: but he that is greatest among you, let him be as the younger; and he that is chief, as he that does serve"* (KJV).

In this verse, Jesus places emphasis on servanthood. Jesus is not taking away the title of leader, He simply changes the definition. The leadership style promoted by Jesus is one in which we serve in love. Since the husband is to love his wife as Christ loved the church, the way he leads will reflect that love. The husband, who is a loving-leader, does not produce misery and misfortune for his wife. The husband operating from this principle is still a benefactor, but he only benefits when others in that household benefits.

God never intended for us to be the dictator or lord over our wives. His plan was for us to lead in a godly way. Jesus set the example for us to follow. Our aim should never be to cause our wives to witness pain, problems, and pressure to have our needs and desires met. This is seen too often in those abusive relationships in which the husband causes the wife to feel second class.

Let's look at some examples that show the differences between the dictator style and the loving style of leadership of husbands.

Dealing with decisions.

The husband using the dictator style of leadership gives orders. He's in charge and that's all there is to it. He makes all the decisions and expects everyone else to just carry out the orders as he directs. He becomes angry and upset when his directives are questioned or challenged. His desire is to have things done his way, and he is not concerned about his wife's opinion on the issue. As a matter of fact, the opinion of his wife or any discussion on the matter is usually threatening to him.

The husband using the loving style is just the opposite. By contrast, he welcomes the opinion of others. He generates discussion on a given subject matter to make sure that he has covered everything. He is willing to listen to his wife's suggestion and combine them with his thoughts on the matter. He is concerned about reaching the right decision for the benefit of the family rather than himself.

Dealing with desires.

The husband who is a dictator has little concern about what turns his wife on as well as what ticks her off. He ignores his wife's God-given desires. He simply makes sure that his desires are fulfilled. It really doesn't concern him that his wife cries over a matter. He usually responds to tears by saying something such as, "There you go with that stupid crying again." When it comes to sex, he treats his wife like a Gomer rather than a gift. Affection is foreign. He simply wants his sexual desires met and is not concerned about hers.

The husband who is a loving-leader seeks to understand his wife. He seeks to discover more and more about her as time moves on. He doesn't view his wife as a sex object but rather the object of affection. He tries to understand his wife as recorded in 1 Peter 3:7. As he seeks to understand her, he applies his understanding in all situations. He tries to fulfill her God-given desires to the best of his ability.

Dealing with differences.

The husband who uses the dictator style doesn't care if there is a difference of opinion on issues. He becomes angry when the wife differs. In his sight, she is being defiant and disobedient by having a different opinion. She is "out of her place" when she does not agree. His wife's opinion is never right because he cannot stand to be wrong.

The loving style respects differences in opinions. The husband who uses this style really believes you can disagree without being disagreeable. He doesn't have any problem with finding out he was wrong and she was right. The loving-leader seeks to find out what his wife's opinion is on issues. She can be a Democrat while he remains a Republican.

Dealing with deficiencies.

The husband operating with the dictator mentality makes it a point to deal with faults, flaws, and failure. He loves to point out the areas of weakness of his wife. He can find fault with everything she does. There is always a point of criticism given when dealing with everything she has done. The food never tastes just right. The house is never clean enough. Her looks are never up to par. He always has some criticism to offer.

The husband who is a loving leader does just the opposite. He seeks to find the good to emphasize and not the bad. He compliments more than he complains. He is aware of faults and tactfully addresses them, if it is necessary, for the benefit of all involved. He spends time noticing things to compliment her about. He notices the new hairstyle and expresses how good she looks. He thanks her for the meal that she spent quality time preparing. He believes that compliments can lead to further construction rather than destruction.

Dealing with duties.

The dictator expects the wife to get the kids dressed, fed, and off to school, work an eight-hour job, keep the house spotless, and meet his sexual needs before she goes to sleep. Since he is the head, he doesn't have to be responsible for any of the duties around the house. Those duties belong to her. He feels his rank gives him a license to be lazy. He even feels that if he takes care of the kids, cleans the house, or prepares a meal, that he should be bowed down to and applauded for his performance.

The husband operating from the loving style tries to help out wherever and whenever needed. He doesn't complain about the dirty dishes but assists with them. He doesn't expect his wife to be the "superwoman" of Proverbs 31 without his assistance. He helps to share the load.

Dealing with denials.

The husband who is a dictator seeks to intimidate his wife when she denies him anything. He tries to prove his manhood by raising his voice or his fist. He physically and emotionally abuses his wife when she does not grant what he requests. He is known to become violent, and this causes the wife to submit in fear of the pain she may receive as a result of denying him.

The opposite is true of the husband who uses the loving style of leadership. He will never verbally or physically abuse his companion. He will not raise his fist during an argument to show that he is a "real man." He loves to use his hands to caress and console rather than to hit and harm.

Husbands must never take advantage of the role that has been assigned by God. God holds the husband accountable for the behavior exemplified. Christian husbands must set the example for the rest of the world to follow. It is also worth noting that a woman can better fulfill her role as a wife according to the Scriptures, when the husband carries out his God-given responsibilities.

It is hard for a wife not to be submissive when the husband is a loving leader. She won't have any problems literally worshipping the ground that her husband walks on when he is on a mission to love her unconditionally. When the wife sees that her best interests are at the top of the husband's list, she eagerly and willingly submits to him.

— Chapter 4 —

The Mysterious Woman

> Learn what turns her "on" as well as what turns her "off."
> Also, make sure you always turn the right knob.

Likewise, ye husbands, dwell with them according to knowledge (understanding), giving honor unto the wife . . .

—1 Pet. 3:7a

The Mysterious Woman

There are some husbands struggling because the woman he thought he knew last month has seemingly changed this month. In order to effectively love and serve, it is important for the husband to know with whom he is dealing. The more knowledge he has about his wife, the more effective he will be in carrying out his responsibilities as a loving husband. This is what the Bible speaks of in 1 Peter 3:7:

> "Likewise, ye husbands, dwell with them according to knowledge giving honour unto the wife, as unto the weaker vessel, and as being heirs together of the grace of life . . .(KJV)".

The Scripture challenges husbands to know what turns her on as well as what turns her off. The husband should understand that even though the wife is made out of the same "stuff" as he, she is still different. The term *weaker* in 1 Peter 3:7 is not pointed out to suggest that she is on a lower level than the husband. It really points to her delicate nature, which requires special care.

There are some clothes that I simply throw in the washer after they have been worn. I place in some detergent, place the washer on a certain cycle, and then turn it on. After the washer finishes its work, I throw those same clothes in the dryer. There is another group of clothes worn by me, however, that I treat differently. Those are the dry-clean-only clothes. They require special care. All of the clothes are important but some require special attention.

The husband is to treat his wife with special care because of how delicate she is. There is no other human relationship greater than the husband-wife relationship. All human relationships are important, and there are certain "cycles" used to take care of those relationships. But the husband-wife relationship must differ from the employer-employee relationship. It must differ from the parent-child relationship. The husband-wife relationship must operate on a plane all by itself with a different set of rules based solely on understanding one another.

My wife is a member of a sorority that uses a hilarious term to identify their husbands. We are lovingly called "Honey do(s)." This label is given because it describes what happens in the home of that couple. When the wife needs something done by her husband, she will say, "Honey, do this . . ." or, at . . ."

As hilarious as this may sound, I believe this is what Peter and others are describing about the husband's role in marriage. The only difference is that we should know and understand what to do without hearing repeatedly from the wife. Not only should there be a "Honey-do" list developed from *living with your wife in an understanding way*, there should also be a "Honey-don't" list developed.

"Honey-Do" List

Do compliment.

Every wife needs to hear her husband say something good about the way she does things. The husband should take the time to compliment the way she looks and the way she does things. Too often, she does things to get her husband's attention; and he never notices, or he notices and never says a word. She should hear from the husband that the outfit she is wearing is beautiful or that the smell of that perfume is breathtaking.

Do cover

The word *cover*, according to Webster, means "something that protects, shelters, or guards". One of the basic needs for your wife is that of security. She desires for her husband to be willing to provide for her as well as protect her. It is the husband's responsibility to make sure that the stewardship program at home is operating properly. There must be control placed on the finances. First Timothy 5:8 reveals: "If anyone does not provide for his own, and especially for those of his own household, he has denied the faith and is worse than an unbeliever" (KJV).

Whether or not the wife is employed outside of the home isn't the point. The husband has been given the responsibility to make sure that he is a provider. The wife should know that the husband has it covered, whether she is employed or not. This of course deals with the basic human needs.

Do continue.

Men, do you remember courtship's smiling days? Remember how you would block out everything else to give full attention to your sweetheart? Remember how you did those peculiar and crazy things, just to spend time with her? Remember how you spent hours on a date, dropped her off, and then you'd call her to talk for countless minutes? All of these were connected to a deep companionship that should continue.

Your wife wants and needs companionship. She desires for you to continue providing quality time on your schedule for her. She was made out of relational substance and must continue to feel that she is important to you. When this is done, you are letting her know that she is just as important to you today as she was when she walked down that aisle and you placed the ring on her finger.

Do confirm.

Your wife needs to know that you really appreciate her unique contributions. So much of what she does is not visible to the masses. This is why Peter says, ". . . grant her honor . . ." When we praise, honor and exalt our wives, it serves as confirmation of her significance and value. If we don't do it, who will?

The confirmation of value and significance comes from those who are in that home with her. This is what Lemuel speaks of in Proverbs 31:28, when he says, "Her children arise up, and call her blessed; her husband also, and he praises her" (KJV). Confirm her value by praising her and honoring her.

Do confide.

A husband's number one confidant should be his wife. She desires to know what is going on in her husband's life. She deserves to know as well. She has to deal with the problems he is facing, whether he shares them or not. There are many husbands who consider themselves protecting their wives by not confiding in them. As honorable as it may appear from the surface, it becomes a tool of Satan, designed to drive a wedge between you and your spouse.

It is better and easier to deal with "us" when the wife is knowledgeable of the things taking place in our lives. Your wife should never have to try to figure out what is wrong with you. She should be told about the trouble on the job. She should even be told about the flirtatious woman who submits her sensuous, seductive suggestions your way. (I will deal with how to handle those a little later in this material). Your wife should never be the last to know. Do confide in her.

Do cuddle.

When you live with your wife "in an understanding way," which really means "according to knowledge," you will spend time cuddling without any ulterior motive in mind. As noted earlier, the husband who is a loving leader never views his wife as a sex object. You should never get to the point where you cuddle simply as a means of foreplay or after-play. Your wife should be cuddled, caressed, and comforted without sex even crossing the corridor of your mind.

Do consult

The last item on the "Honey-do" list is the need to consult your wife. Your wife needs to know that you value her opinion on things. She should be consulted about certain decisions that need to be made. You should always adopt in your union the saying, "Two heads are better than one." When you consult your wife about things, it gives her a sense of value and importance.

Seeking her advice allows her to see that she is not to be a silent partner in the marital relationship. It is important to understand that consultation is designed for confirmation and not confrontation. The reason you want the advice in the first place is for the purpose of confirming whether the decisions you have made are right or wrong. If the opinion differs from yours, it is not right for you to blow up.

"Honey-Don't" List

Just as there is a "Honey-do" list, we should remember that there is automatically a "Honey-don't" list. The opposite of each one listed above would comprise that list of things we should not do. I will not insult your intelligence by making a list of opposites to the above list. However, there are a few things I need to address on the "Honey-don't" list.

Don't neglect.

One problem in marriages I have seen time and time again, is the husband that is so caught up in his job and other extra-curricular activities, that he fails to give his wife the amount of time she deserves. Sometimes men feel that because their wives are sitting in a mansion and driving a Mercedes that they don't feel neglected. This is not the case at all.

Your wife should never think that your occupation is your life. She should never think that she has to play second fiddle to friends and coworkers. She should never feel that she is competing with your hobbies and the sports channel. We should be careful, because neglecting can lead to regretting later on.

Don't suspect.

Satan, the enemy of any institution established by God, loves for the spirit of jealousy to exist in the marriage. He loves for us to listen to others who don't have our best interest in mind regarding the behavior of women. That person who says, "Listen, man, if I were you, I wouldn't give my wife so much freedom to do as she pleases. If I were you, I would make sure she checks in before leaving to go somewhere. If I were you, I would question her about that shopping trip. How do you know she spent all of that time at the mall?"

If you can't trust her, you shouldn't have married her in the first place. Trust is a must in any relationship. If nothing has been done to cause you to distrust her, then you should not suspect her of doing anything wrong. This is one the tricks of the enemy to bring misery in the marriage.

Don't correct (publicly).

There is nothing more embarrassing for a wife than a husband trying to show others that *he wears the pants in his house.* You should never forget that you are dealing with your wife and not your child. She should be treated with respect at all times, especially in public. This is not to suggest that there aren't times when one of you needs to be corrected by the other. Those times will come, but make sure that it is done with love and in its' proper place.

Don't reject.

While "living with your wife according to knowledge," don't reject her sexual advances. There are certain times during the month when your wife can accept the fact that you have had a long day and you are tired. There is another time when her body will not even take that as an excuse. It is how God so designed her. To reject her during this period can be very damaging to her physically and emotionally.

This is why you should learn all you can about your wife's makeup as a woman. When you know that time is drawing near, make sure you are ready to take care of it. God has so designed it so that you won't regret it.

Don't forget.

Don't let anyone fool you. Special days are important to your wife, whether she says anything about them or not. Anniversaries, birthdays, Valentine's Day, and others should not be forgotten. Something special should be done. The husband has a tendency to forget anniversary dates after a while, but this is dangerous! She expects you to remember and do something special. You don't need to buy something that will cause you to file bankruptcy, but please don't forget to do something!

— Chapter 5 —

The Meat and Potatoes Man

> One of the most common descriptions given by wives when describing their husbands is: "He's been acting the same way every since we first started seeing each other!"

And the Lord God formed man of the dust of the ground, and breathed into his nostrils the breath of life; and man became a living soul.

—Genesis 2:7

The Meat and Potatoes Man

When God made Eve, He placed Adam in a deep sleep and removed one of his ribs. After removing the rib from Adam, He began to fashion it into a woman. Can you imagine this event taking place? God takes a small rib and produces a full-grown woman. After creating this vision of loveliness and beauty with all of the wonderful curves, He decided to breathe life into her. When God made man, He took some dirt and fashioned it into a man. After doing this, He decided to breathe life into him. When you compare the way God produced man and woman, the process for creating man doesn't sound as complex and complicated as the process of creating woman. I realize that I am stretching this point. However, I believe the design of man and woman explains the difference in the modes of operation.

As noted in the last chapter, God designed woman as one of the most mysterious of all His entire creations. It takes time to figure out the woman because of her physiological makeup. On the other hand, man is not difficult to figure out. The woman is mysterious and the man is "meat and potatoes." In seeking to please your husband, it is important to remember that his makeup is different from your makeup.

Most men are easy to figure out. You don't have to take a psychology course to understand him. It is difficult to discover a concrete pattern of behavior for women. One day, she may be the most talkative and jovial person, and the next moment, she may give you the silent treatment with little laughter. When this happens, most men try to figure out what they did wrong. In a lot of those cases, it has nothing to do with the behavior of the man, but the makeup of the woman. As a matter of fact, the change of behavior may not symbolize that anything is wrong. She can still be happy and you not know it. God designed her to be this way. God also designed the man to be the way he is. You know when he is happy or sad. You know when he is mad or glad.

With this information in mind, wives can satisfy their husbands by examining some areas that compliment his makeup.

Admiration

Your husband desires to be admired above all others. He desires to be considered the "king of his castle." A husband who is genuinely admired by his wife will not need to seek the admiration of another person. This admiration is seen when the supreme amount of respect is rendered. When his position of headship is honored, he feels admired by the family. He needs to know that his absence creates a void in the home. When he believes he is esteemed highly, he will do what it takes to live up to that image.

Admiration causes the husband to have a sense of worth that is not being received by competing. His admiration in other areas is usually based on "what he does." He has to do a better job than others in the workplace, in order to be admired. He has to be more talented than others in organizations to be admired. The admiration received at home should be based on "who he is." When he is admired just because he is the husband and father, it gives him the greatest amount of satisfaction.

Attention

A husband loves to receive his wife's undivided attention. He understands the wife's association with others; however, he does not want to always be the one at the end of the list. He realizes that attention must be given to children, career, and chores, but he desires to have some time given to him as well. I am not dealing with the selfish husband who desires all of the attention. I am not speaking of the husband who expects his wife to jump at his beck and call. The husband who wants all of the attention does not really understand his role as the husband. I am dealing with the husband that feels neglected when his needs are always placed on the back burner.

A perfect example of the lack of attention received by some husbands can be seen when associating with friends. Most men don't spend a lot of time socializing by phone. They make a few calls to handle business and that is usually the extent of it. Women are different. Since women are naturally relational, they can talk for hours to girlfriends. Although this is a natural thing for women, some husbands have problems with their wives' lack of attention given to them when talking to others. When the phone rings and the husbands says, "I am not going to answer because I know it is for you," it is usually a cry for more attention, or at least, equal attention.

When a husband hears his wife say, "I am going to let the answering machine pick it up so that I can spend some time talking to my husband," this will cause him to see that he is receiving attention over others. There are times when little things are done that cause the husband to believe he is receiving extra attention. For example, my wife will often prepare food for the children and place their hamburgers and fries on a paper plate with paper napkins. When my burger is served, it is on a nice piece of china with a cloth napkin. This may not appear to be much to others, but it allows me to feel like special attention is being given to me.

Appreciation

There are times when husbands and wives take each other for granted. Just as the wife desires to feel appreciated for what she does in the marriage camp, so does the husband. The question should never be: "Why should I say thanks for what someone is required to do?" The answer to the question is simple. When you express appreciation for what someone is required to do, it becomes more of an opportunity rather than an obligation. The husband desires to be appreciated for the things he does. The appreciation expressed should be done privately and publicly. There is nothing worse than a wife expressing appreciation in the presence of her husband and later bad-mouthing him in his absence. In Proverbs 31: 10–12(KJV), we read:

> Who can find a virtuous woman?
> For her price is far above rubies
> The heart of her husband doth safely trust in her,
> So he shall have no need of spoil.
> She does him good and not evil all the days of her life.

The husband in Proverbs expresses appreciation for his wife because he feels appreciated by his wife. When he knows that he is appreciated, he will go over and above the call of duty to take care of his family. When appreciation is spoken and shown, it gives him the emotional support needed to continue providing for his family. He recognizes that providing for his family and securing them is his God-given duty. However, when appreciation is not rendered, it becomes a chore rather than a choice. It becomes a burden rather than a blessing.

The wife should not let a week go by without expressing appreciation for something the husband does. Let him know how much you appreciate the way he takes care of the family. Let him know how much you appreciate him adjusting his schedule to accommodate family above everything else. This appreciation should not just cover the big-ticket items. When he says something like, "Don't cook this evening," or "Let's go out to eat," you should express gratitude and appreciation to him for giving you a break from preparing that meal.

Adoration

The husband wants to be adored by his wife. He wants to know that his wife's world is better because he exists. There is nothing more refreshing to the husband than to hear his wife speak of how much she adores him. In a real sense, although he may not admit it, he likes for his wife to brag about him. When the wife tells others how much she adores her husband, it gives the husband confidence that he is doing what he is required to do as a husband. The expression of adoration should be spoken to family, friends, and the husband as well. The adoration shown to the husband will cause him to show adoration.

Affirmation

The husband expects his wife to be his most loyal supporter. He needs to know that his wife believes in him. Whenever goals are pursued by the husband, the wife must continually affirm him. The affirmation shown by the wife creates determination for the husband. She can make him feel like he can conquer the world or she can make him feel like he is wasting his time. When she affirms his abilities, he will try harder to achieve. He becomes more determined to meet that challenge because of the faith that his wife has in him. The wife can make him feel like he can move mountains.

Even after he fails, she continues to affirm his abilities. She assures him that he still has what it takes to get the job done. She makes it sounds like the company missed their blessing by not hiring him. The more she affirms him, the more confidence he has in his abilities.

Anticipation

The husband anticipates those moments of making love. The sex drive of the man compels him to anticipate having his sexual needs met. His sexual needs differ from his wife. As noted in an earlier chapter, there are times when the sexual desire of the wife is stronger than at other times. The only time when the sex drive is not strong for the average man is usually when he has gone without making love for an extended period. The problem for some men is that they have not learned to combine affection with anticipation. Anticipation focuses in on having the sexual need met. Affection focuses in on the intimacy that leads to the fulfillment of the anticipation. For the woman, the only time when affection is not necessarily required is during that period of the month when she is at her sexual peak. During that stage, she will probably attack you. At all other times, affection is required.

In most cases, the average man has been programmed to anticipate having his sexual needs met rather than being affectionate. Many males have not mastered this emotional display because of its negative image projected by society. God However, has equipped the man with an affectionate side. It usually takes the affectionate wife to pull this unused emotion from him. Once it is uncovered, the average man will do affectionate things on a consistent basis. When the wife romances her husband, the art of affection is being taught, and for the husband, it begins to flow easily. Before long, the anticipation will be coupled with affection. A man needs his wife to help him in this area. Don't allow his anticipation to be denied. Since he has not been programmed to be affectionate as has the woman he may need you to coach him in this area.

Acceptance

Due to the competitive work market, the husband needs to feel like his wife accepts him as he is. On the job, he sometimes feels like he must perform some major feat in order to witness acceptance from other employers and employees. At home, he wants to be himself and feel accepted by family members. He does not want to prove himself or do any special things to be accepted. He does not want to encounter the spirit of competition at home. He desires to be accepted as a man with strengths and weaknesses. As a matter of fact, he should feel that the strengths and weaknesses of his companion create a balance in the relationship.

The acceptance of his weaknesses does not mean that the wife should be satisfied with them. She accepts him as he is and does all that she can to help those weaknesses become strengths. When he is accepted for who he is, he becomes more receptive of the gifts possessed by his wife. He begins to see more and more how blessed he is to have a woman to give balance in the relationship.

Association

Although men do not need male bonding as much as women need other women, there are areas that women need to examine regarding men associating with other men. A lot of men have a built-in competitive spirit. This spirit of competition must be released in an arena other than the marriage. A lot of the hobbies men engage in are designed to address this competitive spirit. Therefore, when they go bowling, golfing, or fishing, it is an attempt to deal with that spirit. This should be encouraged as long as it does not become a strain on the time spent with the family. Many wives do not encourage their husbands to participate in these areas with the fellows. This is dangerous because the competitive spirit must be expressed somewhere and the last place you want to see it expressed is in the home. This association with other men can really be a blessing in disguise.

I remember a woman talking to me years ago about the time when her marriage started going down hill. Her husband had Mondays and Tuesdays off, and like clockwork, he loaded up his truck and went down to the local lake on one of those days with his neighbor. He used one day for special chores around the house and the other to fish with his partner on the local lake. When she got off work, she would pass by the lake on her way home and see his truck. She started complaining about him going to the lake every week. When he would bring the fish home and show them to her, she would complain about him fishing rather than compliment him on his catch that day.

He eventually became frustrated with her consistent complaining about fishing on one of his days off. When she passed by the lake on her way home, she started seeing the truck less and less. After a few weeks, she didn't see the truck at the lake at all. When she would arrive home, she didn't see the truck there, either. As a matter of fact, she didn't have any idea where he was on his off days anymore. In the past, she knew she could find him at home or on the lake. This marriage suffered unnecessary damage simply because the wife had problems with her husband's association with the fishing partner and their fishing expeditions. He actually allowed that competitive spirit to lead to a time of unfaithfulness. Who is wrong in this scenario? Both of them. However, the wife finally admitted that if she had known about a man's competitive spirit, she never would have complained about his fishing expeditions.

If This Marriage Was Made In Heaven,
Why Am I Going Through Hell?

— Chapter 6 —

The Omission of Submission

> Remember that God designed the roles in marriage. Therefore, when we oppose the roles, we are going against the plan of God.

Wives, submit yourselves unto your own husbands, as unto the Lord.

—Eph. 5:22

The Omission of Submission

To Submit or Not To Submit? That Is Not A Question! Before reading the material in this section, I want you to read the following passages of Scripture and ask the Holy Spirit to enlighten your understanding. (KJV)

1. Eph. 5:22–24: Wives, submit yourselves unto your own husbands, as unto the Lord. For the husband is the head of the wife, even as Christ is the head of the church: and he is the savior of the body. Therefore as the church is subject unto Christ, so let the wives be to their own husbands in every thing.

2   Col. 3:18: Wives, submit yourselves unto your own husbands, as it is fit in the Lord.

3. Tit. 2:4–5: That they may teach the young women to be sober, to love their own husbands, to love their children, To be discreet, chaste, keepers at home, good, obedient to their own husbands, that the word of God be not blasphemed.

4. 1 Tim. 2:9–12: In like manner also, that women adorn themselves in modest apparel, with shamefacedness and sobriety; not with broided hair, or gold, or pearls, or costly array; But (which becometh women professing godliness) with good works. Let the woman learn in silence with all subjection. But I suffer not a woman to teach, nor to usurp authority over the man, but to be in silence. For Adam was first formed, then Eve And Adam was not deceived, but the woman being deceived was in the transgression. Notwithstanding she shall be saved in childbearing, if they continue in faith and charity and holiness with sobriety.

5. 1 Pet. 3:1–5: Likewise, ye wives, be in subjection to your own husbands; that, if any obey not the word, they also may without the word be won by the conversation of the wives; While they behold your chaste conversation coupled with fear. Whose adorning let it not be that outward adorning of plaiting the hair, and of wearing of gold, or of putting on of apparel; But let it be the hidden man of the heart, in that which is not corruptible, even the ornament of a meek and quiet spirit, which is in the sight of God of great price. For after this manner in the old time the holy women also, who trusted in God, adorned themselves, being in subjection unto their own husbands.

In the verses listed above, the wife is commanded to submit, to obey, or to be in subjection to, her husband. The idea of the wife's submission is not a very popular one in our day.

First, submission is unpopular because of the mistreatment of women down through the years. There have been many men who have taken advantage of their God-given position as "the head" in the marriage. Consequently, many women have been abused by their husbands because of their warped belief that their wives are slaves and servants rather than partners.

Another reason submission is unpopular is due to the secular definition of the term. The secular definition points to inferiority. There are those who think a submissive wife is really an acknowledgment that she is inferior to her husband. Submission in a spiritual sense is not an implication of inferiority.

A third reason this term is unpopular is due to the spiritual status of people. During this age of the feminist movement, many women have placed the Bible and its principles to the side to follow their own agenda. They want to be "spiritual" without following any spiritual instructions.

The last reason I think the term is so unpopular is due to the idea that the substance of Scripture is based on some time-line. There are many that feel submission was good for the world of the past, but now they feel that God has a different agenda. They view it as gospel truth only for the people in the Bible days.

It does not matter how unpopular the idea of submission is, the truth still remains that it is God's way. All institutions established by God also include specific and detailed instructions to be followed that will cause that institution to operate God's way. We don't have the right to discard anything implemented by God simply because we don't understand it or care for it.

God never intended for the wife's submission to point toward slavery or inferiority. As a matter of fact, submission has nothing to do with any of that. Submission teaches the necessity for order and structure and for a division of responsibility in the home.

We can see in the Scripture that the term submission is always used to deal with organization. The Bible teaches that the church is subject to Christ. It teaches that church members are subject to elders. It teaches that children are subject to parents. And it also teaches that the wife is subject to her husband.

Submission is an act of obedience to the will of God. It provides an avenue for the wife to perform her God-given assignment to make the marriage move in the direction which God intended. It gives the marriage the needed balance required to cause the family structure to be full and complete.

I find it interesting that some women reading the passages mentioned earlier, focus on the wrong things. They will focus in on the apparel, adorning, and the attitude of silence rather than the subject of submission. They will say, "I can wear what I want to wear." Or, "God gave me a mouth to speak, so why shouldn't I?" The area of concentration should be the instructions from God's word to be submissive. Don't major in the minors and minor in the majors.

Let's examine one of those passages mentioned earlier a little closer. In Ephesians 5:22–24, Paul deals with this subject in a very unique manner. Look at what he shares with us about submission.

The Expectation of Your Submission

Paul reveals that God expects the wife to be submissive. Submission is not something the husband created for his own satisfaction and gratification. Paul, who is divinely inspired by the Holy Spirit, says,

"Wives, submit yourselves unto your own husbands, as unto the Lord" (Ephesians 5:22 KJV). Whenever we have His lordship in view, we are dealing with following the instructions of the One who is the director of our lives.

When you view your submission as rendering a service to the Lord, you are more motivated to do it. Doing it for your husband should be secondary. The primary reason behind your submission should be solely because God told you to do it.

The Explanation for Your Submission

Paul next gives the explanation behind these instructions. The reason the wife is to be submissive is because "the husband is the head of the wife (Ephesians 5:22 KJV)". God so designed it this way. He did it for the purpose of organization in the relationship. God desires to have someone in charge. He gave this assignment to the husband.

This is like my position as pastor of the church. I am no more precious in the sight of God than any of the other 3500 members. Although God has designated me as leader of the congregation, all members have been given certain responsibilities and gifts to carry out His program. As the leader of the team, I have the responsibility to equip the saints for service. It is impossible for me to do the job as leader without a submissive team to lead.

The Example for Your Submission

Paul gives us a perfect example to check out. He says, ". . . as the church is subject to Christ (Ephesians 5:24 KJV)". The Christian wife has a pattern to examine. When we look at the family of God, we can see that operating manual comes directly from God. He is in charge of the church. We are to do what He says. The officers of a church don't make up the rules. Christ does! We should remember that the operating principles of the church should not be based on an autocratic or democratic procedure. It is theocratic! We are to do what Christ says rather than what society or people dictate.

The Christian wife's submission is to be just like this. As subjects of Christ, the church becomes more and more viable to perform the task assigned. The submissive wife is designed for the same purpose. God desires for the family unit to become more and more viable in this world of confusion and compromise.

The Extent of Your Submission

Paul reveals that submission, in the spiritual sense of the word, is not to be an on-again, off-again matter or a selective process for the wife. He says she is to submit *in everything*. Submission is not something you do if you feel like it. It is not something that you choose to do based on your view of your husband's spiritual state. God requires that your submission becomes a lifestyle at all times.

The Encouragement for Your Submission

I love the next thing that Paul discloses. He gives the ingredient that encourages a wife to be submissive. It is not difficult for a wife to be submissive when the husband is willing to love his wife as Christ loved the church. This unconditional love is the encouragement needed by the wife to be submissive. This kind of love requires the husband to love his wife even during unlovable moments.

I have discovered in my pastoral counseling that a husband can love his wife into submission. When the wife sees that the love her husband has is so real, she will submit in a spirit of delight and cheer. Think about it. What Christian wife will find it difficult to submit to a man who is constantly giving up his life for her as Christ did for the church? Rick Yohn says:

> A husband who loves his wife as Christ loved the church will make every sacrifice to meet her needs. He will provide for her physical needs of sexual love, financial security, clothes, food, etc. He will provide for her emotional needs like security, affection, understanding, acceptance, the feeling of being wanted, and of feeling necessary to complete him. He will provide for the spiritual needs by encouraging her to grow in the Lord.

The Enablement of Your Submission

I have had many married women to say, "Pastor, I have tried being the submissive wife and I just can't do it." Or they will say, "I know God requires me to be submissive, but it is so hard for me to do." My response to them is always the same. I share with them that in and of themselves, it is impossible to do what it takes to be submissive. But, I also share whatever God commands us to do, He also provides the necessary equipment to get it done.

Isn't it interesting that Paul does not deal with man and his marital, mystical, and material relationships in Ephesians 5 and 6 without dealing with being filled with the Spirit of God first? In Ephesians 5:18, he admonishes us to filled with the Holy Spirit. The only way for the wife to be submissive in everything, and for the husband to love his wife as Christ loved the church, is through the power of the Holy Spirit. He enables us to keep God's commandments.

The Exception of Your Submission

In Colossians 3:18, Paul says, "Wives, submit yourselves unto your own husbands, as it is fit unto the Lord"(KJV). Paul allows us to see through this verse that

63

there are exceptions to the submission principle. If what is requested of you to do is not "fit unto the Lord," you are not to do that.

If you are instructed to do what God forbids, you have a right not to submit. God holds us accountable for the sins we commit. The sinful act is something you will have to answer for. Therefore, there is an exception to a wife submitting when God's commands differ from your husbands.

Chapter 7

The Mean Monster Messing with Married Men

> Some monsters are make-believe in our dreams. Some others are real and you wish they were in your dreams!

Be sober, be vigilant; because your adversary the devil, as a roaring lion, walketh about, seeking whom he may devour.
—1 Pet. 5:7

The Mean Monster Messing With Married Men

Let thy fountain be blessed: and rejoice with the wife of thy youth. Let her be as the loving hind and pleasant roe; let her breast satisfy thee at all times; and be thou ravished always with her love. And why will thou, my son, be ravished with a strange woman, and embrace the bosom of a stranger? (Prov. 5:18–20 KJV)

In this passage from Proverbs, Solomon is trying to give his son, Rehoboam, some advice to help him out in life. He deals with various subjects in chapters four and five that lead him to the right track. In this section, he deals with the laws of marriage. He talks to his son about the need to appreciate the wife that God has blessed him with. He shares the importance of ignoring the "other woman" trap. In dealing with the law of marriage, he addresses the law of morality. He tells him that he does not need the strange woman. In addressing the subject of the strange woman, Solomon tells Rehoboam to watch out for her because of her poisonous ways. He is saying, *Watch out for the mean monster messing with married men!* Her smiles and sweet sayings are subtle, suspicious, and seductive. Her attractiveness and affection are dangerous, destructive, and deadly. Solomon is giving his son an invaluable lesson.

Now, I believe that every word written in the sixty-six books that comprise the Bible serves as the inerrant word of God. It is the inspired word of God. The other thing I believe about this passage is that it isn't just *inspiration* that led to the *revelation* of this divine *information* shared by Solomon. The basis for much of this is experimentation that Solomon knew about firsthand.

I realize that the topic of this section appears to be a case of male bashing. I know that the mean monster messes with men and women who are single and married. The first thing to remember is that this material is addressing the married life and not single living. The objective of this section is to try to reach the married men who are seemingly victimized more than any other by the mean monster.

The mean monster is not the strange woman. The strange woman is the instrument used by the mean monster. The mean monster is really the *strategic satanic substance used to resurrect the monster in us.* The mean monster in us is what the Bible calls the "lust of the flesh" (1John 2:16 KJV). Satan uses the strange woman as an instrument to stir up the lust of the flesh. By the way, the strange woman is not necessarily a stranger. She can be a coworker, neighbor, church member, or family friend. The strange woman is any woman outside of the marital relationship who seductively and sensuously tries to stir up the monster in you.

The mean monster that messed with Solomon's father (David), Solomon, and Solomon's son is still alive and well today. It's still around, lurking and looking. It continues to haunt and hamper men who have dedicated their marriages to God. Many marriages have been ruined because of the invasion of this mean monster.

There is something else you should know about this mean monster. This creature does not possess the regular features of some horrifying-looking monster. As a matter of fact, this mean monster comes in all kinds of disguises. One day it is tall and the next time it may be shorter. One day it can have long hair and the next time short hair. It comes in all sizes. Sometimes it is large. The truth is that it looks like whatever it takes to turn you on. Whatever it takes to stir up the monster in you is the disguise it wears. This mean monster does not cause nightmares (at least not at the beginning). As a matter fact, if you think about the monster long enough, it will cause fantasies rather than nightmares. This monster doesn't just show up in the dark, even though that is where it is trying to take you. This monster will show up on the job, in the neighborhood, at the bank, at class reunions, and yes, even at church worship services.

Many men have not only allowed this monster to mess with them, they have allowed it to master them. It is to the point for some men that they think it is something they can't help. Why are so many Christian men falling prey to this mean monster? Surely, they see how others are now miserable due to the mean monster invading their union. They know what could happen if what is done in the dark is brought to the light.

I believe the reason many Christian men are getting caught by the mean monster is because they don't know how to properly fight it. They have tried to give it a punch here and a punch there, only to discover that the mean monster seemed to increase its' assault. What is there for a Christian man to do to effectively deal with the mean monster? Let's see if we can come up with some helpful hints in handling the mean monster.

1. Run for Cover

The first helpful hint for the man is to *run for cover*! I said "run for cover" and not "*run to the covers*"! Paul writes in 2 Timothy 2:22(KJV): "Flee also youthful lusts: but follow after righteousness . . ."

There are words that change meaning down through the years. A word used in the past could mean something totally different today. The word *flee* in this verse means "Run, Brother, Run!" The meaning hasn't changed. Paul is giving some valuable advice in dealing with the mean monster. He says we should flee.

We must stop thinking that we are spiritual supermen! We are not so spiritual that we can deal with the temptations of the enemy on our own. If you are normal, you need to see how fast you can do the 100-yard dash. You should get out of there. If you go to that class reunion and that "old squeeze" or strange woman shows up and shows out, you had better squeeze your way away from your old squeeze. You don't really need to go to some places without your spouse in the first place.

The only attribute of Superman you need is to be "faster than a locomotive" and get out of there. Listen, if you are tempted and the monster is stirred up in you, don't just stand there and keep telling yourself that you can handle it. If you have to keep saying, "I can handle it, I can handle it, I can handle it," then you probably cannot handle it, so flee.

I have had men to challenge me on this point. They will remind me that we are equipped with power because of our relationship with Christ. They will remind me that the Word of God teaches, "Greater is he that is in me than he that is in the world" (1John 4:4 KJV). I share with those brothers that if the mean monster has been stirred up in you, the greater thing in you at the time is the flesh and not the Spirit of God. I remind them that Paul also writes something else that is helpful here. He records in 1 Corinthians 10:13(KJV):

> There hath no temptation taken you but such is as common to man: but God is faithful, who will not suffer you to be tempted that ye are able; but will with the temptation also make a way to escape, that ye may be able to bear it."

Listen, God wouldn't provide an escape route for you to just stand there and say, "I can handle it.

2. Remember the Covenant

While you are running from the mean monster, it is a good time to remember the covenant you made before the people, the preacher, and most of all, before Providence. When we fall victim to the mean monster, we are breaking the covenant that we made the day we were married. This covenant is not just something we made with our spouses, it is something we made with God.

I believe every couple should memorize the wedding vows. Those words used in that ceremony are not just some beautiful phases used. They really represent biblical truths and commandments of God. When the vows tell us that "you should keep yourself unto her alone, so long as you both shall live," it is representing a commandment of God that says: "Thou shall not commit adultery" (Exodus 20:14 KJV).

When we decide to break the covenant, we are actually breaking the commandments. There are times when we act as though it is all right as long as she does not know. This is the wrong way to view marriage. Remember that God knows.

I remember the first video camera I purchased years ago. I was in the living room of the house, reading the instructions on how to operate the camera. My two oldest sons, who were three and four years old at the time, were watching me work on the camera. Every now and then I would stop working with the camera and start wrestling with the boys. My wife came in and said, "If you boys are going to play, go to the den." I would jokingly say something smart like "Yes, Mother." She left and went to the store. We started wrestling again. While wrestling this time, I broke one of her favorite vases. We knew we were in trouble, so we resorted to the old faithful—Super Glue. We put it back together. Of course, it was not put back together perfectly, but if you turned it a certain way, it looked as good as new.

When my wife returned, we were sitting in the den as though we had been the perfect boys while she was gone. Meanwhile, I had been trying out the new video camera and had finally figured it out. I told everyone to come in to see my first recording. I removed the tape from the camera and placed it in the VCR. As the four of us sat in front of the television, something happened that I will never forget. The picture came on and my wife said, "What is that?" It was a picture of my oldest son Chris and his daddy putting the vase back together again. I forgot to turn off the camera! When we fall victim to the mean monster, we should remember that the heavenly video camera is on at all times. He sees what is going on. God knows our up-risings and our down-sittings. It should also be noted that at some point my wife would have noticed that the vase was broken. Something would have eventually caused her to see the brokenness that had been covered up.

We should get rid of some of these conditions we attach to the covenant. Remember that the vows said things such as, "for better or worse; for richer for poorer; in sickness and in health." We should not commit to keeping the covenant *if* she does certain things. I remember being on duty at a counseling center in Texas once when a couple came in for help. The wife was hurt due to her husband's unfaithfulness but was willing to save the marriage if she could receive a promise from her husband that he would stop being unfaithful. She was willing to forgive him, but the husband wasn't sure he could make the promise.

I looked at his wife, who obviously worshipped the ground he walked on, with tears in her eyes. I found out that they had four beautiful children and she had given up her career to be there for her husband and children. As I listened to them talk, I soon discovered what the problem was. The husband eventually admitted what the problem was. He said, "Preacher, when I married her, she was real thin and that was the thing that turned me on to her. Now she is not as attractive as she used to be." I wanted to say, "Listen you beer-belly brother, she has given you four children and still looks great after those great feats." That's what I wanted to say, but I didn't. I reminded him that he promised to be faithful to her alone unconditionally. I also asked

71

him if he looked like he did eighteen years ago? He dropped his head and said, "No." After several sessions, the marriage was saved. This occurred fourteen years ago, and they still call around their anniversary time each year to tell me that the marriage is great.

The covenant should be taken seriously by both parties. Don't let Satan rob you of your conviction and commitment to this covenant, which is between you and God first, and you and your wife second. Let the mean monster know that you are committed to the covenant.

3. Recognize the Come-On

There are times when we appear to be naive about the things taking place around us. Paul writes about the devil and declares that ". . . we are not ignorant of his devices" (2Corinthians 2:11 KJV). There are certain signs that always surface when the mean monster is at work. There are some noticeable things that will happen to reveal to us that the mean monster is trying to lure us into the trap.

The mean monster will move around you differently from the way she walks around others. There is a dip in her hip and a glide in her stride. It is specifically designed to stir up the mean monster in you. They are trying to attract attention. It is seen in the way she walks, talks, sits, and stoops. It is evident in what she wears and how she wears what she wears in your presence.

You cannot control the "come-on" attempts of the mean monster, but you can cause the "turn-off." The enemy seeks to attract and then attack. The enemy realizes if he can get you to look, then he can get you to lust. This has been one of Satan's approaches from the beginning of man's fall. After he convinced Eve to look, it wasn't long before he convinced her to take of the forbidden fruit.

The answer is not to walk around with your eyes closed. It would be nice if we could get our work done with our eyes closed, but that is not the way it works. The problem is not in *looking* and *seeing*. We have been given the sense of sight for the purpose of seeing. The problem is when we *see* and continue to *look*. Satan knows when the sight becomes an imbedded thought. He can then be more successful in luring us into sinful activity. The more you look, the more ammunition Satan has to trip and trap you. The opposite is true as well. The more you ignore the advances, the less Satan has to use to lure you.

4. Retire the Collection

It is impossible for you to be victorious dealing with the mean monster, carrying your little black-, blue-, or brown-coded book. As a married man, there is no need for you to have the numbers of those ladies of the past. I realize that there are exceptions to this rule. I also realize that the devil loves exceptions. He allows the exceptions-to-the-rules to become a target area for his attacks.

The reason I call it a coded book is because you are allowing Satan to use another one of his schemes called *deceit*. I am referring to the times when you write numbers by certain names to make them appear to belong to someone else. Some men can be so clever with it. They will write the telephone number for Sam and it is really for Samantha, or the name of Joe who is really Josephine. The "just-in-case" collection should be destroyed. Don't just pack it away somewhere. Set some fire to it before it sets fire to you.

Some of you may say, "Well, I got rid of my books a long time ago. I trashed those names and numbers so I wouldn't be tempted." Some people have what I call the "mental Rolodex." They have certain numbers stored in memory. Unlike the book, you cannot set fire to your memory. It is stored there. However, there is a way to get rid of it.

When we had our phone system installed at the church where I serve as pastor, there was a special private line installed just for me. I gave this number to my wife only. Every time my wife called the church, she would call the regular number listed on our church bulletin. One evening, while at home, we tried to call the church, but all lines were tied up except the private line. The problem was that my wife and I forgot the telephone number to the private line because we never used that number. If you want to destroy your "mental roller desk," just stop using the number.

Let me explain why you need to retire the collection. Satan has some special plans in mind to interrupt your marriage. He is waiting for you and your wife to have a disagreement or something. The devil will put Samantha on your mind. By the way, Samantha doesn't really care if you are married or not. You pick up the phone and call Samantha and tell her you just need someone to talk with about your troubles. She says, "You know you can come and talk to me anytime." Satan has just opened the door for you to violate the sacredness of the marriage institution.

5. Refuse the Company
It is important for us to hang out with godly men who are committed to doing things that are pleasing to God. There are times when we will connect with "one of the boys," who seeks to encourage us to notice the mean monster that comes around. This is the brother that you consider a friend who is always using his "built-in X-ray vision."

He is the one who always notices that "hunk of loveliness" and says something such as, "Lord, have mercy."

Be careful in thinking that this won't have any affect on you. Watch out! See the devil knows how well the power of suggestion works. It may not be the strange woman your pal pointed out to you, but after awhile, you start scanning those walking in the mall or in the restaurant on your own. Remember that Satan knows if he can get you to *look at it*; he can get you to *long for it*. It won't be long before you *lust after it* and then the next thing you do is *lay with it*. And, of course, you will eventually have to *lie about it*, due to the fact that you have fallen into Satan's trap.

We must be willing to discontinue our relationship with those who are unwilling to respect our marital status. Satan has enough ammunition to use already to try to lure us into his trap. We don't need to hang out with those who are going to encourage us to do what Satan desires for us to do. It is important for us to express to our brothers that we don't think they should encourage us to look lustfully at another woman. If they continue to do so, we should detach ourselves from their company.

6. Reject the Compliments

Another one of Satan's devices is to use the strange woman to say things to us that we need to hear. He knows if you are not receiving compliments at home, then the strange woman may be able to lure you by simply saying the right things to you. She will compliment the way you are built, the way you dress, the way you smell, or the way you talk. They will say whatever it takes to get you where they want you. They will use those compliments as stepping-stones to higher heights.

Please don't think that every woman who gives you a compliment is the mean monster at work. That is not the case. But there are some clear signs when the mean monster is trying to trap you. When they continuously look you all over and tell you how they love the way that fits, it's probably the mean monster. When they get so close to smell that cologne and you can feel their breath on your neck, that is probably the mean monster. When they desire to touch that material, and the hand moves beyond a simple touch, that is probably the mean monster.

It is important for us to reject certain compliments. You are probably saying, "I don't want people thinking that I am snobbish or rude." It is possible to reject compliments without becoming insensitive to the one making the compliment. The Spirit of God will give us a tactful way to explain how we didn't appreciate the way the compliment was given. But there are those who won't accept tactful ways. Sometimes you have to be stern in what you say to drive the mean monster away.

It is also important to share with your spouse those things you need to hear. Rejecting the compliments of the mean monster is really a symptom of the problem and not the underlining cause. My mother often said something that is appropriate here. She would say, "The good that you do will come back to you." You would be surprised at what will happen when you compliment your wife about those things that you need to hear. She will in most cases do the same thing.

7. Review the Consequences

Have you ever given any serious thought to what could happen if you fall victim to the mean monster? Have you ever thought about the consequences that can come by just committing adultery one time? Do you think that the strange woman desires to remain the strange woman? The answer is that she doesn't unless she does it for a living.

She will one day get tired of playing second fiddle. She wants to move from the second-string lineup to the first-string lineup. She will do things to move her competition out of the way. But, you say, "We have an understanding." It is important for you to keep in mind that this understanding is tainted with sin. The devil will eventually raise his ugly head. When he does, you will see how much understanding exists.

The mean monster has caused a lot of men to fall. I am speaking of men from all walks of life. It has destroyed the lives of men from the president to the preacher. It has wrecked marriages and careers. This mean monster has even taken lives as a result of some fatal attraction or some dreadful disease. Children have become displaced. And the character of some have been assassinated. It can happen to you.

8. Restore the Communion

Listen! It will be hard for you to *run for cover, remember the covenant, recognize the come-on, retire the collection, refuse the company, reject the compliments* and *review the consequences*, if your house is a house of terror. When there is division and discord at home, the devil will use it to lead to sin. The devil loves for a home to lack harmony. He desires for the husband and wife relationship to be impaired to cause his temptations to be more appealing.

When you are spending more hours on the sofa than in the bed, you are giving the devil some rope to work with. When you are sleeping in the same bed but never touching each other, you are giving the devil rope to work with. When you are staying away from home to avoid the hell you are facing there, you are giving the devil some rope to work with. It is your responsibility to work at restoring the communion.

I realize that it takes two to tango. I also realize that it is important for someone to initiate it. There are needs to be met. If you don't allow your wife to meet them, the devil will send the strange woman to meet that need. It is important for us to do what it takes to make sure the fire of love is burning. We should never be satisfied with the fire going out in the marriage. The devil has some matches in his toolbox that he desires to use to light a stick of dynamite to destroy your marriage.

9. Repair the Communication

Without an explanation, it may appear that I have just covered it. But let me reveal what I mean. Communion is an act or instance of sharing. Communication is an act or instance of transmitting information. It is possible to have restored communion and still have problems communicating the way that you should.

You can commune while eating at the same breakfast table, riding together in the same car, or sleeping in the same bed. It is possible to be together without transmitting any information. I realize that a form of communication is taking place here. It is called nonverbal. Nonverbally, you may smile while sitting at that breakfast table. Nonverbally, you sit extremely close riding in the car. Nonverbally, you do some things, other than just sleeping, while lying in the same bed together. If the nonverbal exists without the verbal, you are giving the devil rope to work with.

There is a need for the husband and wife to talk to each other. You need to know what's happening in each other's lives. You need to talk about your feelings concerning various issues. God did not equip us to read each other's minds. You may say, "I may not be a mind reader, but I have known her long enough to almost know what she thinks." You are to be commended for reaching that level. But the key word in your comment is *almost*. Since you cannot be totally accurate, spend time talking to each other.

Many problems can be solved by communicating. Many problems can be avoided by merely talking to each other. Many men have witnessed disaster because that strange woman was someone he felt he could talk to. I have counseled many that would say, "She was someone that I could talk to about anything, and I wish my wife was like that." The truth is that your wife is probably like that. The problem in most cases is that you won't give her an opportunity. Later, I will give some more information concerning communication that will hopefully help you repair the communication.

10. Report the Contacts

One of the reasons you need repaired communication is for the purpose of reporting the contacts. When the mean monster attempts to tempt you, it is a wise thing to reveal this information to your wife. There is nothing wrong with sharing this information with your covenant partner. As a matter of fact, it is probably the smartest thing that you could do.

When your wife is knowledgeable, it helps you to remain faithful. In other words, you don't have to fight the mean monster by yourself. When you have a wife to pray with you regarding the mean monster, you become better equipped to deal with it. Remember that you don't need to have an oath of silence or secrecy in your marriage regarding anything. It is all right to tell your wife what that co-worker did. As a matter of fact, she may be able to give you some good advice as to how you can handle the mean monster.

The problem many men face with this helpful hint is the way some wives respond to the report given. The wife who says, "You must have done something for her to try something like that," is really revealing that there is a deeper problem in the marriage. It is evident that the trust factor is not there or the spirit of jealousy is at work. Some husbands and wives are still having to deal with past failures. In the long haul, revealing the contacts will assist in resolving the problems.

Some men don't reveal the contacts because of the just-in-case scenarios. They allow the devil to plant a thought of not burning down the bridge, just in case there is a desire later on to cross that bridge. And they feel if they reveal it, it could lead to them getting caught later on. Listen, Brother! The devil will keep that on your mind, and eventually you will slip and fall. There is danger in trying to keep the temptation to yourself.

11. Respect the Comments

I believe our wives have a sixth sense about things, including the wiles and ways of the strange woman. They can sometimes see things that we miss. Sometimes the strange woman is subtle in her sensuality. We may not recognize it as it as a come-on. We may see it as something totally innocent. But they may notice something else. I have learned when they tell you to watch out for her, we need to take heed. They seemingly have this radar detector that can pick up certain vibes.

With this spirit of discernment, we should not view the wife as being a jealous mate. I believe God has simply gifted them, so that we can have some help recognizing the come-on. I am not speaking of the woman with the spirit of jealousy that I mentioned earlier. When that spirit is at work, she feels that every woman that speaks to you is after you. This is not the one who is behaving like a gifted helper.

Before you go off the handle, do what Jeremiah said about determining whether a prophet is real or not. He said you can tell the real prophet by evaluating whether the prophecy comes true or not. In most cases, the mean monster will become more bold in her attempts. And you will be able to say that your covenant partner was right. Respect the comments of your spouse.

12. Refuse to Compromise

There are times when we place ourselves in compromising positions. Paul writes to the church of Thessalonica that we should "abstain from all appearances of evil" (1Thessalonians 5:22 KJV). There are certain things that we should avoid doing if at all possible. That innocent lunch with a female can lead to some problems. I had a person once tell me it started with an innocent lunch. "Someone saw us and started wondering what we had going on. All of a sudden, rumors got started around the office, and we ended up making the rumors come true. But it didn't start off that way."

That example illustrates what I've shared about giving the devil rope with which to work. He looks for opportunities like this to employ his schemes. He doesn't mind the innocent intentions as long as they conclude with a guilty verdict. If there is any way possible to avoid going out to innocent luncheons alone, we should avoid it.

Another scene to avoid is when a sister is in need of spiritual counseling from you. There are times when Satan will try to use your Christian behavior against you. Here is a sister witnessing some serious problems in life, and she approaches you. She wonders if she can talk to you for a few minutes after work, or, she calls in distress and reveals how depressed she is over life.

Remember that you can have good intentions, but it is not your intentions that concern me. The devil has something else up his sleeve. I am not saying that we should not demonstrate Christian compassion. I am saying that we should demonstrate that Christian compassion accompanied with Christian caution. I make sure when I receive one of those distress calls late at night never to go alone. I will always call a deacon of the church or an associate minister to go with me.

There are certain activities, affairs, and functions that you should avoid attending alone, if at all possible. In addition, you shouldn't go to the class reunion without your mate by your side. If there are activities that she just can't attend, make sure that you try to avoid "all appearance of evil" (KJV).

13. Run to the Commander and Chief

I started these helpful hints off by telling you to run for cover. We need to run from the mean monster that has won a lot of battles. We need to run from the mean monster that has successfully destroyed many lives. We need to run from the mean monster that has wounded a lot of hearts. We need to run from the mean monster that has wrecked many marriages. You may be wondering, where are we to go when we run? You need to *run to the Commander and Chief.*

See we have someone in our lives more powerful than the mean monster. We have Jesus Christ as our Commander and Chief. When we run to Jesus, He can make the mean monster run from us. This is what James had in mind when he wrote: "Submit yourself unto God, resist the devil and he will flee from you" (James 4:17 KJV). We don't have to give in to the mean monster. We can run to Jesus Christ. He is our source of strength. He can keep us covered and shielded from the mean monster.

There was a group of children playing a game of dodge ball one day in our church gymnasium. The game is set up with a group in the middle of this wide circle. Those on the outside of the circle will throw a ball at those in the middle of the circle. When someone is hit with the rubber ball, the group yells, "Gotcha!" and the person hit is out of the circle. The last one in is the winner. We had this one kid that no one could get out. This kid wasn't all that swift or fast, but he won the game. He was able to win because he had a system. Whenever they threw the ball in his direction, he would simply get behind someone else in the circle, and instead of the ball hitting him, it would hit the one he was standing behind.

Listen, Brother, the devil is throwing his fiery darts in our direction. He loves to say, "Gotcha!" But we have a system. All we have to do is get behind Jesus Christ. He will take all of the blows of the enemy on our behalf. We don't have to get hit by Satan's darts.

I hope these helpful hints will be helpful to you. I presented this information in a church service once and found the conclusion for this lesson. The service was recorded by the video technician. He gave me a copy of the tape. On the label, he put the wrong title of the seminar. Instead of typing, The Mean Monster Messing With Married Men, he accidentally typed, The Mean Monster Missing With Married Men. After thinking about the label, it dawned on me that it was not an accident, but an act of Providence. See, if you apply the helpful hints, the mean monster will *miss* when he tries to hit you.

— Chapter 8 —

I Didn't Think it Would Happen to Me!

> We often say, "The devil made me do it." But the truth is that the devil can't make you do anything without your consent!

Can one go upon hot coals and his feet not be burned? So he that goeth in to his neighbor's wife; whosoever toucheth her shall not be innocent.

—Prov. 6:28–29

I Didn't Think It Would Happen to Me

Many of you, after reading the information about the mean monster, probably are not worried that this will happen to you. Your confidence is probably based on your commitment to God and your spouse. You may be a strong Christian husband or wife. You feel that your spiritual growth down through the years exempts you from the tricks and traps of the enemy in the area of fidelity. Before you become comfortable with those thoughts, let's look at the story of one who was a strong and committed believer. You may reconsider your personal evaluation of this matter.

When you are committed to God, you have no intentions of allowing sin a place on the agenda of the day. You actually pray and ask God to "lead you not into temptation" as you go through the day. You don't get up in the morning and say, "I am going to sin today!" You have no intentions of doing that. On the other hand, Satan has you on his agenda. He is going to set up certain things to cause you not to honor God with your life. The more committed you are, the more ammunition he uses to try to bring misery into your life. Let's look at someone who can really show us how this works.

In 2 Samuel 11:1–15, there is one of the most interesting events taking place in the life of one of the most well known characters in the Bible. The character mentioned in this text was the one appointed by Samuel and anointed by God to become the next king of Israel. The character is the one who had been used by God to slay the giant Goliath. He is noted as the greatest king of Israel.

David, the king of Israel, does something that goes against the will of God. David, one who sought after God's own heart, fell victim to the mean monster working within him. Instead of keeping his eyes on God, he placed them on Bathsheba. Now, he didn't wake up that morning and say, "I am going to lust after Bathsheba today." It just happened. Or, did it? What actually took place to get David in a position to say, "I didn't think that this would happen to me"? What happened to this powerful spiritual man?

Detour from the Duty

In the first verse of this passage, we are told where David should have been. There was a war going on. During this period, whenever there was a war, the king would accompany the troops to a certain point on the battlefield. He didn't fight in the war, but he was there with his troops. The king just didn't sign an order in the oval office, have a presidential news conference, and send troops to fight the enemy. He was there with his troops during any period of war.

According to the text, the troops were at war, but the king was not. For some reason or another, David is not performing his duty as king at this time. David is not busy doing what he is duly obligated to do as king. If you are not busy doing what you are expected to be doing, you are busy doing what you should not be doing. When we are idle, instead of doing our duty, we are looking for trouble. The old cliché suggests that an idle mind is the devil's workshop. I believe that an idle man is the result of the devil working in his workshop.

When we fail to stay busy fulfilling our God-given assignments as husbands and wives, we shouldn't be surprised with the things that take place. There are many couples who were busy doing something other than what they were expected to be doing that led to their fall. If that husband had focused on fulfilling his duty by being the provider and caretaker of his family, trouble would not have come to him. If that wife had been there to fulfill her duty by supporting and encouraging her husband, it would not have happened to her.

Distraction from the Devil

First Peter 5:7 says, *"Be sober, be vigilant; because your adversary the devil, as a roaring lion, walketh about, seeking whom he may devour"*(KJV). When you are not busy fulfilling your responsibilities, the devil will eventually find you. When he finds you, he uses the method that will work best with you. He will create a spiritual setback in your life. He will use distractions to keep you from getting up and performing your duty. David probably asked himself before he went out on the roof why he was there instead of at war with his troops. The devil didn't give him time to put on his uniform and call someone to take him out to the battlefield. He provided a distraction.

The devil will try to distract you further from fulfilling your responsibilities. When the devil shows up, he is not easily detected by how he looks. When Satan comes, he doesn't come as a wild-looking creature dressed in all black with fiery eyes and a deep, loud, chalky voice. Sometimes when he comes, he is actually a "she." If it is tall dark and handsome that you like, that is how he comes. If you like 36-24-36, he will oblige your taste. He uses distractions that will lead to your fall.

David stepped out and saw a vision of loveliness. He looked over and saw his neighbor bathing. Now, David was not a Peeping Tom with a set of binoculars looking for a naked woman. He just looked, and it so happened that the picture of a naked woman entered his peripheral vision. This is really not the problem for David. When you see what you should not see and keep looking, you are walking into Satan's trap. The longer he looked at Bathsheba, the more opportunity was given by Satan to cause this picture of the naked woman to reverberate in the recesses of his mind. The moment he allowed looking to turn into lusting, he sinned.

Defiance of the Decalogue

David had a chance at this point to nip it in the bud. He could have repented for his lustful thoughts and that would have been the end of it. Instead, David sent someone to find out who she was. He learned that she was Uriah's wife. Surely now he would leave it alone because this was a married woman. He didn't stop there. He sent for her.

The Scripture says that he slept with her. The temptation had taken over. Why did David do this? Surely he knew that he was breaking two of the Ten Commandments. He was breaking the ones that say: "Thou shall not covet thy neighbor's wife" (Exodus 20:17 KJV), and "Thou shall not commit adultery"(Exodus 20:14 KJV). The reason David is breaking the law is because of the power of Satan. He knows if he can get you to think it, he can get you to do it.

David could have had any single woman in the kingdom. Why would he sleep with Uriah's wife? I believe it was because he knew it was something he shouldn't have, therefore, he wanted it. I remember that while growing up, we had a neighbor who had a pomegranate tree in her yard. Ms. Wallace had this barbed-wire fence around her back yard. The branches of the tree stretched out over the fence and pomegranates fell on the side of the road. I had been told by my parents and Ms. Wallace never to go in her backyard. One day, I decided I wanted a pomegranate. I stepped over several on the road to get this juicy pomegranate, hanging on the other side of the fence. I slipped and fell and cut my leg on that barbed-wire fence. The scar remains to this day. I was injured attempting to get what was forbidden.

Danger of Depravity

Sin always leads to trouble. All corrupt practices will eventually lead to problems down the road. Your temporary pleasure can lead to problems. Satan will only show us a part of the picture to get us in his web. He never reveals the whole picture, but only shows you the pleasurable side. Remember that sinful pleasure is always temporary, because after verse four comes verse five. Your verse four may have been filled with fun and folly, but verse five will create fright and fear.

David sinned, and the next thing you read is that Bathsheba is pregnant. It is at this point that David starts asking himself, "What have I gotten myself into?" The danger of depravity is always the consequence of defying the Decalogue. As a believer, you are not exempt from the consequences. As a believer, you are not above the law.

One day, while late for an appointment at the church, I was speeding. I knew I had to make it to the meeting because of its importance. As I drove my vehicle over the speed limit, I heard a siren. A Dallas police officer pulled me over. As he approached my car, I remembered how often I saw stickers on cars that said *Clergy*. I remember how this preacher told me that the sticker saved him from getting many tickets. I didn't have a sticker. When the officer told me that he had to write me a ticket for speeding, I looked him in the eye and gave him my spill. I said, "Officer, I am Reverend Karry Wesley, pastor of the Antioch Fellowship Baptist Church." The officer looked at me and said, "So, do you want me to write *Reverend* on the ticket?"

Destruction of Details

The sad thing that happens to people who end up getting into sin is that they make things worse instead of better. David had several opportunities to repent and make things right. Instead, he allowed trickery, one of Satan's tools, to be employed. He sent for Uriah, who was on the battlefield, and tried unsuccessfully to get him to sleep with Bathsheba twice. He wouldn't do it. He sent Uriah back to the battle with a note for the general to put him on the front line. Uriah was killed. There goes another commandment that says: "Thou shall not kill" (Exodus 20:13 KJV). David is on a roll. I realize that sin is sin, but sometimes the cover up is more painful to the faithful spouse than the act

90

of unfaithfulness itself. I have heard many victims say, "But she lied to me," or "He deceived me and tried to cover it up." Yes, it is true that telling the truth does not always resolve the issue. But telling the truth can reduce some of the pain.

Dismissal of Disobedience

After all of this was done, David married Bathsheba. That was a nice thing for him to do. I guess this was done to make things right. He thought that it was over. But remember that unconfessed sin is dangerous. We must never allow Satan to convince us that it is over and done with. We must pay one way or another. Even if your spouse never finds out, you still must pay. Remember that God is aware of everything that you have done. He may just send a Nathan by to reveal that you have sinned (see 2 Samuel 12).

The point that I am trying to make with this message is that David was a strong man of God that found himself trapped in the web of Satan. He didn't mean for it to happen. Each time he did something wrong, he had an opportunity to repent and start over, but he chose not to do it. There is always an opportunity for you to get out of the mess that you got into by simply looking up to God and seeking help.

Chapter 9

Pulling the Marriage Made in Heaven Out of the Pit of Hell

> There is no such thing as problem-free marriage. But if you are a Christian, you know the problem-solver.

My brethren, count it all joy when ye fall into divers temptations; Knowing this, that the trying of your faith worketh patience.

—James 1:2–3

Pulling the Marriage Made in Heaven Out of the Pit of Hell

It is not good that the man should be alone; I will make him a help meet suitable for him.

—Gen. 2:18

I know what happened. You spent time in prayer and God sent you a Christian mate to unite with in holy matrimony. You spent time thanking God for this godly man or woman that He provided for you. On that wedding day, as she walked down the aisle, you said to yourself, "I have finally found the one to spend the rest of my life with." She appeared to be the best thing that ever happened to you. She was everything you wanted in a woman. I mean you did some serious looking before making this commitment and concluded that he or she was that God-sent mate.

It seemed to be great for a while, and then all of a sudden, it appeared as though the bottom fell out of the marriage. Now you are trying to figure out why you are going through so much hell in what you thought was a marriage made in heaven. "Since he or she was the one, why isn't there more bliss than burdens? Why isn't there more glory than gloom? Why isn't there more joy than jealousy? Why isn't there more trust than trickery? Why isn't there more intimacy than insults? Why isn't there more fondling than fights? If this marriage was made in heaven, why am I going through so much hell?"

There are many Christian couples who feel as you do. Things just didn't move in the direction that they thought they should have when they exchanged vows. The danger is that many interpret the present gloom to mean that it wasn't made in heaven in the first place. But if you prayed and received God's direction in the beginning about this relationship, and He confirmed it, it was made in heaven. God hasn't changed His mind about the mate he sent your way.

Many Christian couples have become a number in those sad divorce statistics because they felt the havoc in the marriage led to it. Remember that the Bible teaches us in Luke 16:18 "What therefore God hath joined together, let no man put asunder" (KJV). Therefore, the answer is not for you to get out of the relationship because things are not going the way you think they should. There are many that have done this without God's blessings. Instead of life being filled with meaning, it is filled with misery. Well, what is a husband or wife to do about it? Should they continue despite the way things are? Are they to be satisfied with their lot in life and just continue as usual? The answer is yes! You need to continue to do what is necessary in bringing about satisfaction. If it didn't start off in hell, it doesn't have to stay in hell. There are some things we can examine that will help you to climb out of the marriage "hell pit."

The Satanic Invasion

We must remember that this institution called marriage was established by God. Therefore, Satan is going to do all that he can to invade the premises. He tries to interrupt anything that God approves. He doesn't mind that you are married, he just desires for you to be miserable in the marriage. Satan has invaded the marriage when there are more glimpses of gloom rather than glory.

The sad thing is that we permit him to do what he does. As believers, we have been given power and authority over the devil. In Luke 11:1, we read, "Then he called his twelve disciples together, and gave them power and authority over all devils. . . (KJV). We don't have to give up anything to the devil. We need to learn how to stand boldly on the Word of God and reclaim what belongs to us.

We must use the God-given right (authority) and ability (power) in relation to our marriages. We must let the evil one know that he can't have the marriage, nor can he drain it of its joy. God never intended for us to be miserable or unhappy. The devil loves for us to walk around depressed and disgusted. But we must not give him the victory. When he attempts to enter God's territory, we must take a stand. When my oldest son Christopher was a toddler, he would enjoy inflicting pain in my life. When I would hold him, he would take both of his hands and playfully hit me on the face. He had big hands and they would hurt. Every time he

95

hit me on the face, I would say, "Ouch! Chris, that hurts." The more I said those words and frowned, the more Chris would laugh and continue. The next time he did it, I didn't say ouch, and I laughed at him. When he discovered that I was not reacting the way he wanted me to, he climbed out of my lap and found his mother's face and lap.

You will be surprised at Satan's reaction when you refuse to allow him to bring misery and pain into your marriage. He will flee. When my wife and I recognize the enemy trying to invade our heavenly camp, we laugh at him and let him know that we are aware of his attempts. When he gets tired of us laughing at him for long periods of time, he will leave us alone.

We need to have more of a David-style religion when it comes to our boldness. Remember when Goliath was attacking the armies of God, David took a stand. He said, "What is this uncircumcised Philistine doing taunting the armies of the Lord?" (1Samuel 17:26). When Satan invades our camp, we must put him in his place. We must inform him that he is barking up the wrong tree. We must rebuke him.

You can't keep Satan from invading the premises, but you can let him know that you won't give him the victory. By the way, he will not stop invading the premises simply because you didn't fall for his tricks. What he will do is leave; and if he came with a .22 caliber weapon, he returns with a .38 caliber weapon. But remember that the Bible said that "No weapon formed against you shall prosper . . ."(Isaiah 54:17 KJV).

The Secular Input

I am an advocate of seeking counsel to deal with our marriages. Proverbs 12:15 says, ". . . he that hearkeneth unto counsel is wise" (KJV). But I also believe we must be careful in what counsel we accept. There are times when we allow our minds to absorb some of everything as a means of dealing with the marriage that is witnessing problems. There are times when we are so desperate; we will try to apply whatever we receive to end our marital blues. We must be careful about selecting what we listen to, as well as look at, as a means of addressing our marital problems.

There are times when we mentally receive what we see happening on television as counsel. As Christian couples, we must not allow the ways of the world to serve as the example by which we operate our marriages. For too long, we have allowed the things we see happening in Hollywood and romance novels to serve as the measuring tape for our unions. We spend too much time listening to unchurched people in the workplace giving advice to us regarding this institution established by God. We are quick to apply the suggestions and ideas of the secular marriage experts who never mention what God says about marriage.

The Hollywood movie is just that, a movie. As believers, we should not focus on the latest number one movie as the way our marriage should operate. When that movie was being made, the director was able to say "Cut!" when the movie wasn't flowing the way he thought it should flow. There were several retakes done before you receive the finished product. Remember those persons you see on the screen are not really husband and wife. They are actors and actresses being paid for their performance.

There is also a problem when we operate our marriages according to Oprah, Montel, Geraldo, Rickie Lake, or Rolando. There are times when we look at these talk shows and hear something that sounds like our situation. We then allow what we hear on the talk show to serve as the answer in dealing with the problems we are facing in marriages. We fail to examine certain components in our relationship that differ from what we are watching on the show. Remember that Rickie Lake is more concerned about the *ratings of the show* than the *remedy of the situation*.

We should not seek the solution for our problems from those who are not in agreement with us spiritually. If they are not Christians, don't expect them to put you on the right track. I believe that there are many marriages that ended up in divorce court because the couple received the wrong counsel. They listened to the wrong people, and were told that there was no hope. They received ungodly advice from ungodly professionals. Please don't expect secular input on the spiritual institution of marriage to bring you out of the marriage hell pit. There is a need to find professional Christian counseling to help you through your problems.

The Scriptural Instructions

Don't expect to move out of hell's pit and up the heavenly ladder without any heavenly instructions. Too often, we try to apply the best-selling marriage enrichment book formula rather than the Word of God to our problem marriage. The problem some married couples have is that they have become so indoctrinated with secular ideals that they prefer them over the Word of God.

We can find the answer in God's Word. We should take out time to examine what God says about His subjects first. If you really want to get rid of the problems you are facing in the marriage, you must apply the Word of God to it. God's Word serves as our message, measuring, and method book.

The Word of God serves as the message book to man.
It tells us what it is that God desires for all of us to know. He gives us messages covering several areas, including the area of relationships. He deals with material relations, mystical relations, and marital relations. We must receive His message on the subject before we try other means.

The Word of God serves as a measuring book.
We should not spend our time comparing our marriages to other marriages. When we compare, we can always find a marriage better or worse than ours. We should use the Word of God as our measuring tape. We should compare the way we are conducting our marital relations to what the Word of God teaches.

The Word of God also serves as our method book.
If we want the marriage to move in the direction that God intended for it to, we must allow the methods found in the Word of God to become our operations manual. It is only when we allow the principles of God's Word to exist in our marriages that we can climb out of the hell pit.

We must remember that the Word of God never becomes outdated or antiquated. I realize that we are living in the age of feminism and machoism, but the principles of the Word must still be applied in order for it to work the way God planned for it to. When the Word of God is rightly understood and judiciously practiced, then you will see that the marriage made in heaven is filled with happiness.

We must be careful when receiving the message the world offers. For instance, when the Bible speaks about the wife being submissive and being under subjection to her husband, the world says that is male chauvinism. But the Word of God is designed to bring harmony into a relationship and not hardship. His instructions are to be followed as given.

The problem is that there are many just taking a part of the prescription rather than the whole. Many husbands and wives fail to understand that submission and subjection are not terms implying that the husband is superior and the wife is inferior. This is simply the divine order that God has given for the institution of marriage. It is designed more like the pilot relationship mentioned earlier. God has placed the husband on board the jet of marriage as pilot, but the plane can't fly without sharing the controls with the copilot. Failure to do so will lead to the plane crashing.

I suffered with a serious sinus infection some time ago. I went to see my physician and he prescribed two medications to deal with the problem. I was instructed to take all of the medication for a period of two weeks and the problem would cease. One of the medications had a terrible taste. The other did not. I was to take the medications three times a day, yet I took the medication only when I remembered to do so. Two weeks passed and I still had the problem. Upset, I was about to call my doctor to ask him where he received his degree to practice medicine. I was going to let him have it. Just as I picked up the phone, my wife picked up my medication and showed me something that changed my philosophy of life. She pointed out the following words on the bottle: "For the best results, follow the prescription."
Listen, if we want our marriages to flow the way God intended, we must follow the prescription. We can't take some of the medicine and not the other if we desire to witness healing. God designed the institution of marriage that way. It is not hard for a wife to be submissive when the husband is willing to love his wife "as Christ loved the church." For the best results, let's follow God's Word.

The Stormy Interruptions

There is no such thing as a problem-free marriage. Too many couples enter marriage with what I call a fairy-tale mentality. This "happily-ever-after" philosophy soon leaves after the first disagreement arrives in the marriage. Even though we are talking about a Christian man and a Christian woman uniting in marriage, problems will still come. There will be some stormy moments to come.

Think about what the Bible describes happening when you are married. The Scriptures reveal that the "two shall become one flesh" (Genesis 2:24 KJV). The two, who have become one, bring differences into that state of oneness. They bring different personalities, different perspectives, and different pasts. When you have many differences brought into a marriage, there will be difficulties along the way.

You may say, "Well, I should not have married someone so different from me." Believe it or not, that really is not the problem. One of the worse things we could do is marry someone just like ourselves. It will lead to a compatible marriage and also a catastrophic one. William McRae writes in his book, *Preparing for Your Marriage*:

> Marriage is not a partnership of two identical people. What could be more self-destructive than the union of two perfectionists or two totally impatient persons! Some similarities in personalities repel each other as common poles of two magnets. True incompatibility is not two unlike persons being able to tolerate each other's strengths and weaknesses, but rather two similar people unable to adjust to a personality identical to theirs.

It is not a question of whether or not there will be a storm; the question is when those storms come, what will you do to resolve them? It is necessary to deal with the storms as they develop rather than just sitting back hoping they will pass over. Failure to deal with the little storms can lead to some major storms down the road.

We should seek to resolve those issues and bury them. The devil loves for us to have unresolved problems. He realizes that unresolved storms will cause the marriage to go down deeper into the pit of hell. As the problems surface, we should sit down and try to talk through them. Failure to do so will lead to future problems remaining unresolved. It's like that couple that sought counseling, and the husband said to his pastor, "Every time my wife and I have an issue to deal with, she becomes historical." The pastor responded by saying, "You mean 'hysterical,' don't you?" He said, "No! I mean historical. She is always bringing up things that happened years ago." It is hard to deal with the present storms and prospective storms when you haven't released the past storms.

The more we learn about each other's differences, the better we are able to relate to each other. The first part of 1 Peter 3:7 points this out. He writes that husbands should live with their wives "according to knowledge, giving honour unto the wife . . ." (KJV). There is a need to live with each other with an understanding of one another. The husband and wife should dwell together with understanding. We must seek to understand those differences and operate accordingly. We need to know what turns our spouse on as well as what turns him or her off.

The Speaking Impediments

It is important to learn how to speak to one another about the issues that develop in the marriage. Proverbs 15:1 says, "A gentle answer turns away wrath, but a harsh word stirs up anger" (KJV). A lot of the problems we have in our marriages can be corrected by simply talking to each other. There are so many couples who can't sit down and "talk through" what is going on. They are always allowing the shouting match to take place.

We must be selective in the words we choose when speaking to one another. The words we choose can determine the route in which the relationship is going. We cannot allow the devil to keep us from resolving marital issues simply by speaking the wrong language. We must learn to speak words that heal rather than hurt; words that comfort rather than condemn; words that praise rather than punish; and words that are soft rather than sharp. We must learn how to speak to one another.

Another speaking impediment that exists is when we limit our speaking to very few words. The Bible says, "He knows the imaginations of our thoughts" (1 Chronicles 28:9 KJV). The Bible is speaking about God and not our mates. It is important for husbands and wives to stop expecting the other person to be able to read their minds. There are times when we expect our spouse to automatically know when something is wrong. We use the excuse that he or she should know by now that something is wrong, since we have been together for so long. Is this really a fair assessment? Even if he or she should know, wouldn't it be easier to just express what the problem is?

The hectic schedules that exist can sometimes cause speaking impediments. When you have so many irons in the fire, it may be necessary to schedule some special time to have a talk-back period. This may sound like an unusual way to communicate to your spouse, but why should you have to schedule time to talk to each other? Well, the answer is really simple. You make time for all other important things. You schedule time to complete work assignments. You schedule time to take the kids to their extra-curricular activities and time to participate in those hobbies you enjoy. Isn't your marriage just as important? With all of the other things that you have on the schedule, your wholesome communication with your spouse can easily get lost in the shuffle.

The Side Influences

This is one of the most hell-producing elements that you can allow to exist in your marriage. When you have outside influences from people on his side or people on her side, you can expect difficulties to come. I am not speaking of the professional Christian counselors that we talked about earlier. I am speaking of in-laws, coworkers, and so-called friends. I am speaking of people who only listen to one side of the story and then reach their conclusions. I am speaking of those who may have not been in favor of the marriage in the beginning. I am speaking of people who use their experiences as the only expertise in dealing with your problems.

It is possible that those who are sharing advice with you have good intentions. Sometimes the advice given is good. The only problem is that they may have received the wrong information. We must remember that in many cases they may be partial because "he is my son," or "she is my daughter." You should not expect the divorced coworker to encourage you to stay with your wife or husband.

When the Bible says, "For this cause shall a man leave his father and his mother and shall cleave to his wife," I believe that also means that we should not go running back to our parents when a problem surfaces in the relationship. When we "leave" and "cleave" as a couple, we are making a commitment to try to work through our problems as a married couple rather than calling Mom and Dad. There are times when parents can give solid and spiritual advice. When this happens, it should be when the couple seeks it, and not just the parent's offspring.

It is a good thing to watch out for those comments that start off with "If I were you, I would . . ." First of all, remember that he or she is not you. Second, the advice about to follow those words is usually based on something that he or she has witnessed in the past in one of their relationships with someone totally different from your spouse. Last, a real counselor gives valuable information for you to make up your own mind.

The Same Ingredients

Another reason you may be questioning your marriage now is because of how things are different in comparison to the way they were before you exchanged vows. During courtship's smiling days, things were great. You miss those moments when certain things happened to keep the fire burning. You miss the romancing, flowers, little notes, walks in the park, and just sitting around the fireplace hugged up.

What happened to the fire that once burned in the relationship? It is like the relationship was traveling on the *Loveboat* en route to Fantasy Island, and all of a sudden the ship wrecked on some deserted island without any hope of being rescued. What is a couple to do when the relationship has seemingly lost the excitement that once existed?

I remembered something that happened to me as a child. One cold wintry day, my father lit the fire in the fireplace and gave me instructions to keep wood on the fire so it wouldn't go out. I started looking at television and forgot all about the fire until I started feeling the temperature changing in the den of our house. I looked in the direction of the fireplace and noticed that there was no fire. All of a sudden my father walked in, and I approached him with tears in my eyes. I confessed that I let the fire go out because I was completely absorbed in what was happening on television.

My father patted me on the head and then walked toward the fireplace. He put a couple of logs on the fire and walked away. I thought maybe he was going to get some matches and some paper to start up the fire again. He then sat in his favorite chair. A few minutes later, I looked in the direction the fireplace and noticed that the fire was burning again. I asked my father how he was able to start the fire without matches. He told me that the fire had not really gone out. It was just covered by the ashes from the burned wood. It needed some additional wood placed on it.

I believe that if the fire really burned in the past, it can burn again. As a matter of fact, I believe that the fire is probably still there but covered under the ashes of what I call the marriage-maturation process. There are other things that came with the covenant of marriage that kept your attention while the fire was slowly dissipating. There were things like careers and children that came along that may have diverted your attention. These diversions may have affected the relationship to the point that the draft in the air is now felt by you and your spouse.

All you need to do is put some logs on the fire and the fire can burn again. It is necessary for both to be involved in putting the logs on the fire if the romantic temperature is to increase in the relationship. There is not a special or new kind of log needed. All you need to do is pull from the log pile that you used when the fire was really burning. You can still send the flowers, write little love notes, cuddle around the fire, and go to the movies. You will be surprised. Your spouse isn't really looking for anything new. He or she is simply looking for some fresh water from the old well.

The Spirit's Involvement

The most important element needed to bring your marriage out of the hell pit is the power of the Holy Spirit. All marriages made in heaven come equipped with a special agent to provide special roadside assistance. When your marriage, like your vehicle, stalls by the side of the road because of a flat, fuel problems, or a bad battery, you can call AAA. Or in this case, the third Person of the trinity to help you. There are times when we try everything but the right thing to save our marriages. We must follow the instructions of Matthew 6:33: "But seek ye first the kingdom of God and His righteousness and all these things shall be added unto you" (KJV).

It is God's desire to save your marriage. He is waiting to help if you would only allow Him. Turn the marriage over to him. Pray for your wife! Pray for your husband! Pray for God to direct you in doing what it takes to make the marriage work. Ask God to reveal what is needed to change the direction in which the marriage is moving. I should warn you that God will not always point the finger at the other person. Sometimes God will reveal that we are not doing things according to His will. He shows us areas where we need to make improvements.

The Spirit of God will allow His power to help in the marriage if we will allow him. There are times when our marriages are filled with so much difficulty that we allow it to affect our relationship with God. We wonder if God is there for us. It appears as though God has abandoned us in our time of distress. The relationship with God appears to be just as distant as the relationship with your spouse.

A friend of mine, Charles Martin, told a very interesting story that serves as an illustration. There was an older couple driving behind a younger couple one day. The young couple in the front car sat all up under each other as they drove down the road. Every now and then, the young husband in the front car would lean over and kiss his wife. The wife in the other car said to her husband of many years, "Honey, we used to do that. What happened to those days?" The husband driving looks at his wife and says, "Baby! I am still in the same place. You moved over!"

God is still in the same place. We may have moved over. But there is some good news. The Bible says in James 4:8 "Draw nigh unto God and He will draw nigh unto thee," (KJV). Go ahead and move back over and allow God to work wonders in your marriage.

Chapter 10

Spiritual Warfare: The Wedding Wedge

> When we fail to get past the past, the beauty of the present cannot really be experienced.

Therefore if any man be in Christ, he is a new creature: old things are passed away; behold, all things are become new.
—2 Cor. 5:17

Spiritual Warfare: The Wedding Wedge

It is my opinion that all Christian couples planning to get married ought to be required to read certain books. The one that is at the top of the list for me is really not a book about marriage. I believe that every couple should read Neil Anderson's book entitled, *The Bondage Breaker*. You may ask, why would a book covering spiritual warfare issues be required reading for couples getting married? One of the most over-looked issues facing Christians today is connected to our fight against Satan.

Throughout this book on marriage, I have talked about devious devices of the devil designed to destroy what has been divinely done. Satan is determined to undermine what God desires. He will try all of his schemes to cause us to be miser-able in any area that is of God, including marriage. A lot of his tricks are not implemented once we exchange vows. Don't think that Satan waits to go on the warpath when we decide to get married. He has already been busy in our lives long before then. He causes many to enter marriage with what I call the "wedding wedge." He causes many couples to enter the institution of marriage already separated.

The story is told about how an elephant trainer works with elephants to get them to do what he wants. The story actually begins when the elephant is young and the trainer has placed chains around one of the elephants' legs. It is a strong chain that causes the elephant to stay in place. Every time the elephant tries to move, he feels the pressure of the chain and remains in place. The elephant keeps trying over and over again. At a certain point, the elephant stops trying to get away, because of the strength of the chain.

As the elephant gets older and bigger, the trainer has to remove the chain from the leg of the elephant because the strength of the elephant is greater than the strength of the chain. The trainer is not worried about this. The trainer realizes that the elephant will not move because of the "chained mentality" that exists. The elephant never realizes that he is no longer bound, due to the attempts to get a way that failed in the past. He is really a free elephant with a slave mentality. A lot of the luggage we bring into the marriage is connected to past guilt. We allow the behavior of the past to serve as a wedge for the future. When you confessed your sins to God and asked Him to forgive you and save you, He did just that. He took everything that was sinfully done and forgave you. Your slate was clean at that moment. Satan, however, wants you to hold on to those past acts. He desires for you to feel guilty about them for the rest of your life.

The Word of God teaches us that "you shall know the truth and the truth shall set you free" John 8:32 (KJV). The truth is that the past cannot have an affect anymore in your life. You have been given the victory through Christ Jesus. The truth is: "If any man be in Christ, he is a new creature, old things are passed away, behold, all things have become new" (2Corinthians 5:17 KJV). Those old things have been forgiven and now you are brand new.

Christians don't realize the freedom they have gained through Jesus Christ. They don't know who they are in Christ. This lack of knowledge has caused many to enter marriage with a load that they really don't have to carry any longer. There are unresolved issues from the past that still linger. These issues can cause Satan to possibly have a stronghold in one's life. I believe that unresolved past pain and guilt could affect your present pleasure. It could affect everything from the consummation of the marriage to the communication in the marriage.

It is possible that there are past relationships that we have possibly even hidden deep down within that caused us severe pain. If we did not deal with it properly, the ramifications will be seen down the road. These past relationships are not just limited to the other guy or the other lady you dated that did some horrible things to you. Some of that past pain could be connected to your parents, siblings, church staff, baby sitters, and so on. If you don't deal with the past and witness the freedom available through Christ, Satan will use it to produce pain for you as long as he can.

There are those who were sexually, physically, or emotionally abused as children who are still carrying the weight of that abuse around with them. Even if the abuse was short-lived, the pain of it is still there if it hasn't been properly addressed. There are times when you forget about the pain, until something happens to stir it up for you.

111

It is not easy to let go of the pain and pressure associated with our past. Failure to do this will create unnecessary pain for those who are connected to us in the present. I have had countless counseling sessions with persons trying to figure out what was wrong with their marriage. They couldn't pinpoint anything that happened during the period of dating or in the marriage that caused them to feel so down and depressed with their marriage partner. After many sessions, it was soon discovered that there were people in the past that did things that caused them not to be happy in the present relationship. The husband or wife had really done no wrong. It all stemmed from the past.

You may be wondering, *What should be done to deal with the pain of the past? What good would it do to allow those things to surface mentally? Why should I deal with it, since it took years for me to push those negative feelings down?* Every thing just mentioned is why you should deal with it. If the pain of the past still produces pain, it is not in the past. As much as you try not to think about it, Satan will allow things to happen so you will not forget it. If you have suppressed the pain, it is still there and must be removed.

I preached a sermon some years ago on Mother's Day entitled, "A Mother's Love." Following the sermon, a very strong and active member of the congregation, who was at the time separated from her husband, came into the office in tears. I knew that her mother passed away several years ago, and I assumed that she was sad like many of us who no longer had our mothers around to enjoy. I remember saying to her, "Just thank God for those days He blessed you to have her around. Remember all of those good days and just rejoice." After I finished with that stupid spiel, she said, "Pastor, I hated her so much. She would beat me almost every day. Even while I took care of her while she was sick, she would curse me out daily."

After scheduling several sessions with her, we discovered that the problems in her marriage were really connected to the bitterness she had in her heart against her mother. After she forgave her mother, the marriage was restored.

In Neil Anderson's book, The Bondage Breaker, he gives the "Seven Steps to Freedom" that all believers should go through. All of the steps are important. The one that I have discovered most helpful in marriage counseling is the one dealing with "Bitterness verses Forgiveness." Every couple should take an inventory of the past to see if there are persons who wronged them that they need to forgive.

If This Marriage Was Made In Heaven,
Why Am I Going Through Hell?

— Chapter 11 —

Communication:
The Key to Problem Solving

Communication is the "Master's" key to unlocking all doors in a marital relationship.

Let no corrupt communication proceed out of your mouth, but that which is good to the use of edifying, that it may minister grace unto the hearers.

—Eph. 4:29

Communication: The Key to Problem Solving

I have read several books that talk about communication as the key to a successful marriage. Although I agree whole-heartedly with them, I believe, however, that we should take it a step further. Communication is not only the key; it is the master key that unlocks all of the doors. Communication is able to unlock every door in the marriage. It unlocks the door to problem solving, intimacy, and romance. It unlocks the door to God-given roles. It fits all doors.

Since communication is the master key that works, why are there so many marriages in trouble? Communication is difficult for many people because they were unintentionally indoctrinated (not to communicate) while growing up.

We live in a very technological age. This age has its advantages and disadvantages. I am grateful for the technology that exists. The material in this document actually took just a few weeks to pull together, due to the modern age of computers. The old way would have taken me a few months with the other responsibilities I have in my life. So please understand that I am not knocking this technological age. But think about the way things once were.

There was a time when most people didn't have many mechanical communication "blockers." The blockers are the gadgets that we have two and three of in our homes, such as televisions and telephones. There was a time when families would sit around and talk to each other because they didn't have a television, or there was only so much that you could watch. When they did watch television, families watched together in the same room. Now in the average home, you have two to three televisions, including the one in the bedroom.

Hectic schedules we now have also serve as communication blockers. The nine-to-five commitment to the job is almost history. The average full-time employee will invest an average of ten to twelve hours a day with the job, and this does not always include the commuting time. These hours consequently affect the time spent with the family. If you leave home at 7:30 A.M. and return at 7:30 P.M., it will soon be time for the children to go to bed so that they will be fresh for school the following day.

The wife, who may serve as the domestic engineer, is just as exhausted as the full-time employee who spent ten to twelve hours at work. A lot of what she desires to get done can't be done until the children are asleep and dinner is over. It was difficult to take care of it during the day because of the attention she had to give to the baby in the family. She was unable to prepare everything on the menu because of the major unexpected interruptions that developed. The toddler decided that he wanted to repot the plant in the living room. Consequently, the carpet is now a mess and almost ruined.

On the weekend, you need to complete things at home that you couldn't accomplish during the week. Tasks to do include repairing the sink and mowing the lawn, oil change for the car, and trips to the grocery store or cleaners. And, there are the Saturday Little League games. You feel guilty about missing the extended services of the church that took place during the week, so you go to the Saturday youth meetings to volunteer.

Everything taking place in your life is important. The problem is that sometimes we become so busy "doing" that we actually stop "being." We stop being the attentive, understanding husband. We stop being the loving and caring wife. It's not something you intended to happen, it just happened because of the communication blockers. It happened due to the increase in your responsibility. Your plate is full; you have too many irons in the fire. You have to work, purchase groceries, and you must get involved in extra-curricular activities with your children.

How is communication to flow when so much is happening? What can be done to make sure that we are "being" and not just "doing"? Well, it is true that you cannot stop doing the things that are necessary for the family. But there are some adjustments that you can possibly make in the schedule to address the communication blockers. You must do what it takes to ensure that effective communication happens. This is needed in the husband-wife relationship as well as the parent-child relationship.

One suggestion is to produce some "television blockers." Commit to a time of not watching television. The family should implement some special family games that cause communication to take place. Sometimes for instance, block all televisions but one, and, as a family unit, watch television. You will be surprised at how much wholesome communication takes place, simply because you are watching television together.

Another thing that you can develop and implement to produce wholesome family communication is what I call the Brady Bunch Plan. I once marveled at the way Mike and Carol Brady ran their household. Although I realize that we are dealing with Hollywood, I still believe some of the things on the show can work in the real family. At least one episode per week consisted of the Brady Bunch having a family conference. This was a time when the entire Brady family met to discuss various issues. At most of the meetings, all were able to express their opinions. At some of the meetings, Mr. and Mrs. Brady called all the shots.

One thing you can do to address the husband-wife communication blockers is to find special times to get together. When the husband and wife can have lunch together, do it. This serves as an excellent time to communicate, possibly while the children are at school. Although this is not always easy, especially when you work miles away from each other, it can be done. The old saying, "If there is a will, there is a way," is appropriate here. I know one couple that will take only thirty minutes of their one-hour lunch break for three days a week in order to have two long lunch breaks to spend with each other during the week.

It is also good to compare and coordinate schedules for the upcoming week. This can be a great Sunday evening exercise. Several things happen with this exercise. One is that communication is taking place. When you spend time talking about the different activities scheduled for the next five to seven days, you are transmitting information, another way of communicating. You are sharing information.

Another thing that can happen with this exercise is that you can possibly find some time for each other and get it on the agenda. If you have that time designated to take your wife to the movies or out to lunch, it is no longer free time to schedule anything else. I am aware of one couple who have coordinated their schedules in such a way that their break periods on the job take place at the same time so that they can use that time to talk to each other by phone daily.

There is one more thing taking place with this exercise that is probably one of the most powerful components of a marriage. It is called openness. You are actually revealing your life for an entire week to your spouse. You are being open about the things you do. The wife or the husband is able to see that you are not spending time away from him or her intentionally. They are able to see you are not producing communication blockers on your own.

There are some key ingredients needed to communicate effectively. Let's look at some special projects couples can exercise to master communication especially in the area of problem solving. The projects that are about to be discussed are not listed in any specific order.

Project K.I.S.S (Kindness Involves Speaking Softly)

The Bible says, "A soft answer turneth away wrath; but grievous words stir up anger" (Prov. 15:1 KJV). Have you ever said something when you were upset that you wish you had not said? Sometimes the words spoken and the way they are spoken can add to the fire. It is extremely difficult to have a successful conversation when people are yelling and screaming to the top of their lungs. The problem cannot be resolved because the goal of each spouse is to get louder than the other. It becomes a debate that becomes "sound focused" rather than "solution focused."

I always encourage couples to take several deep breaths before speaking. This can have a calming affect when you're upset. If you don't like people yelling and screaming at you, it is wise to practice what you desire. You should always take time to think about how something will sound before it is stated.

Project M.E.A.N.
(Mandatory Emotional Adjustment Needed)

Proverbs 14:29 says, "He that is slow to wrath is of great understanding: but he that is hasty of spirit exalteth folly" (KJV). It is important to have an "attitude check" before trying to resolve an issue. When your emotions have taken over, it can lead to disaster. If you are thinking negative, when you speak it will come out negatively. There are times when couples must take a timeout. You need to take out time to adjust your emotions. When your emotions are overwhelmed by what has happened, it is sometimes difficult to deal with the problem. Go for a walk, or enter into your secret closet. Take out time to calm down.

When the timeout is taken, make sure you do things that will not intensify the problem. I know one person who used to take her timeouts by going to the mall. Whenever her husband caused her to become upset, she would go to the mall to calm down. She claimed that she had to do this in order to adjust her emotions to talk to her husband. When she went to the malls angry, she would spend money and run up the charges on the credit cards. After going on this spending spree, she calmed down. After the husband saw her enter their home with the merchandise, he had to take a timeout to deal with the excessive spending. The wife did not realize that she was taking her frustration out on her husband by making him angry about the spending.

The best way to use your timeout is to enter your secret closet of prayer. When we pray, we should ask God to make the necessary emotional adjustment needed. God knows how to calm us down when the devil tries to cause us to do something sinful.

Project A.N.G.E.R. (Asking Nicely Gets Effective Results)

Proverbs 17:27, 28a says, "He that hath knowledge spares his words; and a man of understanding is of excellent spirit. Even a fool, when he holdeth his peace, is counted wise. . . ." (KJV). In counseling sessions, I have witnessed spouses exploding without giving the other spouse an opportunity to respond. In most of those cases, the explosive spouse discovered later that a mistake was made by not allowing the other to speak. It is impossible to get down to the bottom of the issue if you don't know what the issue really is. Many people explode before trying to find out what happened. In most cases, if you take out time to find out what actually took place, it will probably keep you from exploding.

A tactful approach is the best way to go. When issues surface, ask your spouse about them in the nicest way possible. Kindness begets kindness and yelling begets yelling. Too often, I have heard people say that if they would have known what really happened, they would not have acted the way they acted. If you want to know, politely ask.

Project W.A.R. (Words Affect Resolution)

We have addressed how you should say what you say. Next, we need to address what you say when you speak. "Pleasant words are as an honeycomb, sweet to the soul, and health to the bones" (Prov. 16:24 KJV). Paul says, "Let no corrupt communication proceed out of your mouth, but that which is good to the use of edifying, that it may minister grace to the hearers" (Eph. 4:29 KJV). The words we use can help and heal or hurt and hinder. As believers, our words should always be pleasant. The devil knows that the words selected can serve as additional fuel for the fire or water to put the fire out. He prefers that we use words that pierce and puncture rather than heal and help. If you don't deal with your anger properly, *corrupt communication* can flow from your lips. And the old cliché is not true which says, "Sticks and stones may break my bones, but names will never hurt me." Words can hurt. We shouldn't allow any unholy words to flow from our mouths. Proverbs 12:18 says, "Reckless words pierce like a sword" (KJV).

There are times when we say things and wish we hadn't said it later. One of the things that I have heard happen again and again is name-calling. When name-calling takes place, it will lead to an explosion. I always encourage couples to vow never to say anything to anyone that they would not like stated to them. You should practice what I call "spiritual speech therapy." This involves thinking about what you are planning on speaking before you speak it. Ask yourself, "Would God be pleased with what I am about to speak? Would I like for someone to say what I am about to say to me? What is the best way to say what I need to say in a spiritual way?" After you have asked these questions, more than likely, your words will be as sweet as a honeycomb.

Project S.T.E.W. (Scheduling Time Eliminates Wars)

Most of the disagreements that surface in a relationship are the results of not spending enough time communicating. One way to prevent emotional stewing is to make sure that you schedule communication time everyday. Every spouse should plan on setting up some special time daily to giving the other spouse "a good listening to." When couples go for days without sitting down and addressing the events that have occurred in life, it leads to issues stacking up in the relationship. When issues stack up, you end up going through a period of unstacking the issues to figure out what is wrong.

This could be avoided by simply scheduling time daily to address the current events taking place in each other's lives. It is important to take interest in what the other is doing. Take out time to ask questions to initiate conversation. When you know of special activities taking place, ask questions about them. Ask questions like: "How was your day? How was the seminar? How did the interview go? Did the baby do anything to make you laugh today?" When couples schedule time to share, it will not be difficult to find time to deal with issues that may surface.

Project T.E.R.M.S.
(Truth Expressed Resolves Matters Swiftly)

Proverbs 12:17 says, "He that speaks truth shows forth righteousness; but a false witness deceit" (KJV). Proverbs 13:5 says, "A righteous man hates lying: but a wicked man is loathsome, and cometh to shame" (KJV). Lying is always sinful and dangerous. There is never a justifiable reason to tell lies. A member of the church where I serve challenged these words of mine. He said, "Pastor, What if a man carrying a .38 caliber pistol came to the church door looking for you while you were teaching Bible study? Would you like for me to tell him the truth about your whereabouts or would you prefer I lie?" I said, "I would prefer that you do neither. I would like for you say, 'Run, Pastor, run!' " There are always consequences to lying.

Issues can't be resolved unless the truth is spoken. The devil is pleased when we lie. He doesn't mind us communicating when the information we transmit is filled with deceit. There are times when we try to cover up some wrong that we have done. Just talking about it won't correct it. The truth must be spoken. Prov. 28:13 says, "He that covereth his sins shall not prosper: but whoso confesseth and forsake them shall have mercy" (KJV). As a Christian husband or wife, you have been commanded to tell the truth. Sometimes telling the truth involves admitting that you were wrong and your spouse was right.

There are times when we speak a lie and don't define it as a lie. Have you ever had your spouse to notice something wrong with you, and when he asked if anything was wrong, you respond by saying, "Nothing is the matter?" You just told a lie. There is something going on and you won't talk about it.

I realize that sometimes telling the truth can be painful. Although the truth can be painful, it is always less painful than when the truth is learned after a lie has been told. Yes, it takes time for people to deal with the truth. It takes much longer to deal with a lie. Communication involves telling your spouse the truth. It should not be sugarcoated or exaggerated. You should say it straight. At first, it may lead to some uncomfortable moments. In the long run, it will work to your advantage. Once the truth is spoken, you are able to address the real issue rather than a bunch of false issues.

Project S.W.A.P. (Speaking Without Addressing Problems)

There are many people who think they do a great job communicating because they talk a lot. Communication involves swapping conversation. Proverbs 10:19 says, "In the multitude of words there wanteth not sin: but he that refraineth his lips is wise" (KJV). Proverbs 13:3 says, "He that keepeth his mouth keepeth his life: but he that openeth wide his lips shall have destruction" (KJV). Proverbs 18:13 says, "He that answereth a matter before he heareth it, it is folly and shame unto him" (KJV). Some people have not figured out why God created us the way He did. He gave us one mouth that opens and closes. He gave us ears to remain open at all times. I believe He intended for the mouth to be closed at times, so that we can listen only. Although the ears remain open at all times, if we talk nonstop with our mouths, we will not be able to hear. Sometimes the best way to resolve issues is not based on what you say but what you hear. There is a time to speak and there is a time to be quiet, so that someone else can speak. James 1:19 says, "Be quick to listen, slow to speak and slow to anger" (KJV).

We must be willing to listen to the other person talk. There are times when we say it all without taking out the time to listen. It disturbs me when we expect people to listen to everything we have to say, but we will not give them the same opportunity to speak. When you listen, it requires your undivided attention. You are not really listening while looking and concentrating on the Dallas Cowboys' next play. You are not listening when you are trying to make sure the fingernail polish is put on the nail and not on the finger.

Good listening also requires that you take out the time to make sure you really understand what the other person is saying. My wife's interactions with our boys illustrates this concept. Whenever she is speaking to the boys about something, she will ask them to explain what she just said. Of course they may not repeat what she said verbatim, but she can tell if they really understood it. If there is no clarity in what you are saying, you are wasting your breath. After someone has spoken to you about something, it may be good to respond by asking them, "Are you saying . . ." "Do you mean . . ." "Let me make sure I understand . . ." You can save some valuable time in the long run.

Couples should take time to listen to what the other has to say. We cannot address the problems that develop in marriages without taking the time to hear. The best way to communicate is to swap information.

Project S.T.E.P. (Spend Time Effectively Praying)

Proverbs 16:1 says, "The preparations of the heart in man, and the answer of the tongue, is from the Lord" (KJV). Sometimes it is hard to say what needs to be said. Sometimes it is difficult to figure out how to resolve the issues in a marriage. It is important for believers to spend time in prayer. James says, ". . . the effectual prayer of a righteous man availeth much" (Jam. 5:16b KJV). The best way to assure that you say the right thing is to spend time in prayer. The Lord will prepare your heart and cause you to say the right thing.

As you pray to God, I recommend another project that I call Project R.E.A.D. (Record Every Answer Disclosed). When we seek God's help, He will reveal things to us that we probably had not considered. Sometimes He will show us several things that are going on in the marriage. After the issues have been recorded, seek God's remedy to the problem. His remedy usually involves reading the Scriptures and applying what is written to the problem. For each recorded answer, try to find Scriptures to help you. After this is done, it will be good for you to sit down with your spouse and discuss them.

A strong prayer life is important. When we spend time effectively praying, God will speak to us. One of the results of spending time in prayer is the revelation of truth. God will sometimes show us more than we expected. There are times when He will reveal negative things about us that led to some of the problems we may be facing. It is important to record those things so that you can discuss them with your spouse. He will speak through His Word. Proverbs 13:13 says, "Whoso despiseth the word shall be destroyed, be he that feareth the commandment shall be rewarded" (KJV). Proverbs 3:6 says, "In all thy ways acknowledge him and he shall direct thy path" (KJV).

Project F.R.I.E.N.D. (Finding Resolutions Immediately Ends Negative Dispositions)

Proverbs 15:13 says, "A merry heart maketh a cheerful countenance: but by sorrow of the heart the spirit is broken" (KJV). It is a dangerous thing to place your problems on the back burner. When Paul wrote, "Be angry and sin not", he immediately dealt with giving the devil a foothold (Eph. 4:26–27 KJV). When we refuse to deal with a problem that has surfaced in the marriage, we give the enemy an opportunity to drive a wedge into the marriage bond. The longer you allow a problem to go unresolved, the more difficult it will be to live harmoniously with your spouse.

It is important for married couples to take out time to resolve the problem as soon as possible. One of the proverbs that I despise is the one that says "Love means never having to say I'm sorry." One of the reasons for prolonged marital storms is connected to this saying. Since neither spouse is willing to apologize, it becomes difficult for marital bliss to exist in the relationship. I think a better proverb to use in marital relationships would be: Love means never having a problem saying I'm sorry. The power of an apology is amazing. The emotional disposition will be noticeably different once the apology is given.

It is hard for a person to confess to wrong when he or she believes that forgiveness is not possible. As Christians, we

127

must be willing to forgive each other for the mistakes we make. The devil desires for us to hold on to our bitterness. He realizes that when we are unwilling to forgive, it not only affects our relationship with our spouse; but it also affects our relationship with God. We must be willing to seek forgiveness as well as give it.

Project D.E.P.A.R.T.
(Don't Ever Publicly Address Relationship Turmoil)

Proverbs 15:23 says, "A man hath joy by the answer of his mouth: and a word spoken in due season, how good is it!" (KJV). Have you ever gone to a public function and witnessed a married couple arguing over their problems? Have you ever attended a family gathering on Thanksgiving or some holiday and ended up having to serve as the referee for married couples discussing their problems at the dinner table? When there is a problem, don't deal with it in public. There are times when issues are dealt with in the presence of family and friends and embarrassment follows.

There is a time and place to deal with all issues. It should always be done in private. It may be necessary to pull your spouse to the side and ask if you can deal with the issue when you get home. I also encourage couples to avoid dealing with certain issues in front of their children. There are some topics of conversation that children should not hear. I think some problems should be dealt with in front of the children so that they will learn how to resolve problems. This should only happen when the married couple has matured to the level of resolving issues without losing their composure.

Project D.R.O.P. (Denying Reality of Problems)

Proverbs 12:25 says, "Heaviness in the heart of man maketh it stoop: but a good word maketh it glad" (KJV). One of the worse things to do is to deny that problems exist. Many couples ignore the presence of problems and in turn never resolve any problems. Some feel if they deny the existence of the problem, it with somehow magically vanish away. They soon discover that the heart becomes heavier every time they ignore the existence of a problem. It is a proven fact that our bodies are affected physically by refusing to deal with problems that surface in life. Ulcers, stress, blood pressure problems, and heart attacks, sometimes occur because people are trying to ignore the presence of problems.

Married couples must accept the fact that the problem will not go away by ignoring its existence or hoping for it to disappear. When a problem exists, confess it. Not only is confession good for the soul, it is good for the heart and stomach, too. I encourage couples to tactfully reveal when they have some concern. You should approach your spouse and express your concern about an issue. Whenever you repress the problem, it will always get worse before getting better. When you confess it and express it, you can resolve it, and give that heavy heart a break.

Project H.E.L.P. (Handling Every Lingering Problem)

Proverbs 11:14 says, "Where no counsel is, the people fall . . ." (KJV). Okay, you tried all of these suggestions and the problem still remains unresolved. It may be necessary for you to get some help from a third party. When problems continue to linger in the relationship, it is usually a sign that a counselor is needed. Counseling is not a bad thing. There comes a point when couples may need the assistance of a strong Christian counselor in order to resolve the problems in the marriage.

There are times when the marriage partner will use excuses for not seeing a counselor. Some of the most common excuses are: "We can deal with this ourselves." Or, "I don't want anyone else to know our business." Or, "I don't think we have a problem" (D.E.N.Y.). With all of these excuses, the fact remains that there is a problem. It is probably true that you could deal with it, but you haven't. A real counselor has taken an oath of confidentiality. I have discovered that some couples have allowed certain problems to linger for so long that they have literally become comfortable in their misery. When help is needed, it is important for the couple to find someone who will not be partial to either. It is important for the couple to agree on who this will be.

Project F.A.C.E.
(Fatigue Affects Communication's Effectiveness)

Proverbs 3:24 says, "When thou liest down, thou shalt not be afraid: yea, thou shalt lie down, and thy sleep shall be sweet" (KJV). Let me paint a scenario here. You worked twelve hours and came home and prepared dinner. Your husband is working the evening shift and will arrive home at midnight. You took the kids to the youth meeting at the church after checking to make sure their homework was done. After making sure the children have taken their baths, you tuck them in for the night. Now that the children are asleep, you can catch up on some of the dusting and laundry.

It is almost time for your husband to come home, so you go and warm up the meal you cooked earlier. You greet him at the door, and after preparing for bed, you go and give him a kiss goodnight. He stays up for another hour and comes to bed. You are just about to doze off to sleep, and he says, "We need to talk about the house we are saving for and the amount of money being spent on luxuries." The lights are turned on and you slowly sit up in the bed to address a problem. As he is talking, you feel like yawning, but you try everything in your power to resist it. Since you are focusing on "yawn resistance," you really can't concentrate on what he is saying. If you yawn, he will feel like you are not taking him seriously. You listen and nod periodically in agreement because you can't wait to place your head back on the pillow.

Has the issue really been resolved in this scenario? Has the couple effectively communicated? The issue probably was not resolved because fatigue hinders one from communicating effectively. Whenever I use this scenario in one of my seminars, I ask couples what they think would have been the best way to address the issue. One person said that the husband probably should have ignored the issue. Another said that the husband did right because Ephesians 4:26 says that we should not go to sleep in our wrath. Another said that the wife should have made a cup of coffee and stayed up all night, if necessary, to resolve the issue. All of these responses are interesting, however, I think the answer is related to what I call Project R.E.S.T. (Rest Eradicates Satan's Trap).

The enemy knows that when we are mentally and physically exhausted, it is difficult to resolve a problem. Furthermore, he knows that any attempt to do so will probably cause the situation to get worse instead of better. When you are exhausted, you will sometimes say things that you don't mean or remember. Rest is needed to deal with this issue. There are several things that should have taken place. First, the husband should have asked the wife about her day. After finding out about the events of her day, he should have introduced the issue. He could have said, "Honey, can we spend a little time talking about the budget and how we are going to get our new home, before you go to work in the morning." This gives the husband and wife an opportunity to get some rest before dealing with an important issue. After resting, your brain is better able to transmit information.

Project S.M.A.R.T. (Sex Made After Resolving Trouble)

No one desires to have problems in a marriage, however, it is inevitable. Problems are going to come. When you learn to effectively communicate, the quicker you will be able to resolve the problem. Making up after a problem has been resolved can offer the best lovemaking episodes that married couple will ever witness. The quicker you resolve it, the quicker you can make up. Solomon says, "My beloved spake, and said unto me, 'Rise up, my love, my fair one, and come away. For, lo, the winter is past, the rain is over and gone'" (Song of Sol. 2:10–11KJV). When the winter is over, look forward to the springtime of intimacy.

In conclusion, when communication flows properly, we can prevent a lot of quarrels and arguments from occurring in the marriage. The better we communicate, the fewer problems we will have. Proverbs 17:14 says, "The beginning of strife is as when one letteth out water: therefore leave off contention, before it be meddled with" (KJV). In other words, "It is hard to stop a quarrel once it starts, so don't let it begin."

— Chapter 12 —

Sex: The Last Chapter

> Never let the sex drive move from "tri-weekly" to "try weekly" to "try weakly."

Marriage is honourable in all, and the bed undefiled: but whoremongers and adulterers God will judge.

—Heb. 13: 4

Sex: The Last Chapter

One of the reasons many marriages face difficulties is the subjection to sexual urges occurring in earlier chapters of the relationship(s) than God intended. Many have mistreated the temple of God by experimenting sexually before marriage. God produced sex for married couples only. It is out of the will of God for couples to engage in sex outside of the covenant of marriage. How can you deal with the urges? You deal with it just as you deal with any other temptation, you "submit to God, resist the devil and he will flee from you" (James 4:7 KJV).

Sublimate means "to divert the expression of (an instinctual desire or impulse) from its primitive form to one that is considered more socially or culturally acceptable". The spiritual equivalent of sublimation comes in Jesus' teaching: "whoever finds his life will lose it, and whoever loses his life for my sake will find it" (Matt. 10:39 KJV). Sexual and emotional energy can be harnessed by Christ and directed toward His goals. Loving, serving, and caring all take energy. So does using our gifts and abilities for the good of others.

Changing the Sacred Terms

Sex was designed for married couples only! There are no exceptions. Periodically, I encounter the couple who seeks counseling before marriage that has decided to live together before exchanging vows. I have caused many to become angry with me because I refused to provide spiritual counseling when the couple has decided to transgress the law of God by living together and engaging sexually before marriage. They even try to justify why they are doing it. I have heard every excuse imaginable. They will tell me: "Since we are getting married in the near future, we feel it is okay to live together." Or, "We thought if we started working on our budget by combining bills like rent and utilities, it was okay to live together before we actually exchanged vows." Or, "Since we had a child out of wedlock, we thought it would be good for the child if both parents would dwell in the same place until we were ready for marriage." Here's my favorite, "We thought that it would be good to try out our compatibility in living together to make sure we are compatible in all areas."

The Word of God will not support any of those reasons that you may label as justifiable reasons to engage in sin.

When we intentionally transgress the laws of God, we permit the devil to get a disastrous foothold in our lives. Your body is the temple of God; it is God's dwelling place. When you engage in sex before marriage, you are in a spiritual sense, polluting God's dwelling place. I realize that this sounds harsh, but it is true. Since our bodies belong to God, and He does not give us permission to engage in sex before marriage, do you know what we are doing? We are raping the temple of God.

I took a survey a few years ago of approximately fifty teenagers between the ages of fifteen and eighteen, attending a seminar. This was a group of young people from various churches. They were asked to spread out around the room and to fill out the survey forms without writing their names on it. After completing the survey, they were to place the responses in a box. (The survey only involved putting a mark by a certain response on the survey form. Therefore, they didn't have to worry about their handwriting being recognized.) One of the survey questions asked was:

Have you been sexually active: _____ Once
_____ Twice _____ More than Twice _____ Never.

I will not give you the results of the entire survey. But I will tell you that only 40% placed a check mark by the "never" response. Isn't that an alarming statistic? Over 60% of those young people had already engaged in sex. An act created by God to be enjoyed by married couples has already been experimented with by so many youth today. What is going on? Why are they committing this sinful act at such an early age?

My oldest son had problems saying words that started with the letter t when he was younger. His t always sounded like a d when he spoke. One day, at age two, still learning to pronounce and enunciate, he said that he wanted to watch the television. When he said it, however, he added a syllable, and said he wanted to watch the "devil-vision." We have to admit that one reason our youth are being sexually active the fact that we are living in what I call an X-rated society.

Everything has a sex-appeal message attached to it. The movie industry feels that it can't produce a picture without some type of sex scene in it. Commercialism almost always allows some form of sex appeal to sell a product. Our young people see all of this happening, just as we do. The devil takes advantage of this and allows thoughts to be planted in their minds. They start thinking that sexual involvement is a natural thing that should occur anytime rather than waiting until marriage.

Satan is implementing his plans early. There was a time when children didn't have certain things on their minds at such a young age. But now you can have questions asked by six and seven year olds that will literally knock you off of your feet. This is because Satan has increased his assault. Satan has started indoctrinating us at an early age, to think if it looks good, it must feel good, so just do it. Or, he tries to get one to think that everyone else is doing it, and if I am not doing it, something must be wrong with me.

I can use my six-year-old son Karl as an example of how Satan desires to start early with our children. One day Karl (six) and Chris (seven) were in the den watching television, while my wife and I sat in the kitchen. We heard some giggling going on as they were watching. One moment they would be talking loud and the next minute they were silent. This was unusual, because they were always talking loud. So I peeped around the corner and discovered why they were giggling at times and silent at other times.

They were watching this television show called *Bay Watch*. Their eyes were glued to the television as ladies walked on the beach in their bikinis.

I waited until a commercial came on (the commercial was more alarming than the show), and I stepped from around the corner. "What's up boys?" I asked. "Nothing much, Dad," was their response.

"What are you guys doing?"

"Just watching a little television," was Christopher's reply as he started reaching for the remote control.

I then asked Karl, "What are you guys looking at?"

"We are watching this picture about some life guards."

"What's the name of the show, Karl?" I asked.

Without thinking about it, a Freudian slip occurred. He said, "*Babe Watch*."

Combating the Satanic Traps

Since we know that Satan is going to do his part in trying to teach that premarital sex is okay, we must combat his lies by revealing the truth. We can no longer wait until they reach adolescence and talk about sex (and not the birds and bees), we must get busy telling the truth. The truth also involves dealing with realistic consequences. If they are able to learn that premarital sex is wrong, they will understand later on that extramarital sex is wrong as well. We need to move beyond the biological elements and teach them spiritual truths. Yes, we should teach them biology, but let's also include some theology. They need to know about the human anatomy, and we cannot leave that up to the school system to teach. I have often been asked if I am opposed to sex education classes in schools. My response is always the same. "I am opposed when that is the only sex education they have received."

We must change this "if-it-feels-good-do-it" attitude that exists. There are too many young girls who have lost something sacred by operating from this philosophy (their virginity). We must do something to change the route that we are traveling. We need to teach them to save themselves for their husbands. As crazy as it may sound, that Christian man who is looking for a wife would love to have someone who has saved herself for him.

A friend of mine named Willis Johnson tells this story to stress what a man really desires in the woman who will become his wife.

> When a man goes to purchase clothing that is packaged, he will do some strange but interesting things. Let's say it is a shirt he's after. He will look for what he thinks he wants. He will find an opened package. He looks at the color, size, shape, and texture of that article of clothing to see if he likes it. He may even try it on to see if he likes the fit. When he decides what he wants after taking the aforementioned steps, he will take that opened package, put it back down, and get an unopened package to purchase.

It is the unopened package that the man is after. Too many young ladies have been "tried on" and "tried out" only to be placed back on the shelf, while an unopened package is chosen. We need to have young ladies to commit to remaining "unopened" until their wedding day. This is the way God intended for it to be. He is pleased when He can find someone like a Mary (the mother of Jesus) in the time in which we live.

You may say after reading this, "I guess it is too late for me now, since I have already engaged in sex." That is not necessarily true in a spiritual sense. You can still change.

I love what committing one's life to Christ does. The Bible says, "If any man be in Christ, he is a new creature; old things are passed away, behold, all things have become new" (2Corinthians 5:17 KJV).

I have a friend who works for a major manufacturer. He has a very interesting job. Whenever you purchase some of their merchandise from a local retailer, you receive a warranty for the product. The warranty assures you that if you are not pleased with the product, during a certain period you can return the used-but-undamaged product for a full refund. The local retailer will then place the used-but-undamaged product back on the floor to be sold. The customer will usually look at the opened, undamaged-but-used product and decide to purchase an unopened package of the same product.

This is where my friend's job plays an important part. When the used-but-undamaged item is returned by the retailer, he has the responsibility of receiving the item and making sure it is in good shape. He then sends it back to the retailer in a brand new package. All of the parts have been resealed. It looks brand new.

You may have been used in the past, but when you go back to the Divine Manufacturer, you can be checked out and re-packaged. God gives us a fresh start. Now save yourself for the honeymoon!

Cherishing the Special Time

My two oldest sons and I were playing basketball one day, and all of a sudden, I heard Karl say, "Oooh! Chris! You said a bad word."

I said, "What's wrong Karl?"

"Daddy! Chris said a bad word."

"What did he say?" I asked as I watched Karl with his hand over his mouth.

"Daddy, "I'm not going to say it."

"Go ahead and tell me, " I said. "You won't get in trouble."

"Chris said that Mommy can't play with us, because she is the wrong sex."

After laughing for a minute, I allowed that time to become what I call a teachable moment. I convinced Karl that the word *sex* used in any context is not a bad word. I went on to explain in a very simple way that how people treat the subject of sex can either be right or wrong. There was only so much I could share with a six and seven year old that made sense. I did what I could.

There are many like Karl who have allowed Satan to create this thought that the word *sex* is a bad word, when it is not. When God produced it, He never intended for it to become negative. And the Word teaches us that "Every good gift and every perfect gift comes from God" (James 1:17 KJV). It is not bad. It is "umm-umm good." The way we have allowed Satan to pervert the subject is bad. God intended for sex to be good.

God never intended for sex to be just for procreation purposes only. He designed it for the husband and wife to witness pleasure with each other. I feel this is another aspect of God making the man and the woman *suitable* for each other. As a matter of fact, when we examine the Creation story, sexual pleasure is emphasized before we hear anything about "be fruitful and multiply" (KJV). In Genesis 2:24, we read "For this cause shall a man leave his father and mother and shall cleave to his wife and the two shall become one flesh."

The idea of becoming "one flesh" refers to sexual intercourse. It says nothing about becoming one flesh for the purpose of having children. That comes later. It is alluding to the pleasure of sexual intercourse. This is why the next verse says, "the man and the woman were naked and not ashamed." They were happy. It was a pleasurable thing for the husband to look upon the nakedness of his wife. It was a pleasure for the wife to look upon the nakedness of her husband.

Curing the Sexual Timidity

"Since it was designed to be a time of pleasure, why are there husbands and wives who loathe the very thought of making love with his or her companion?" you may ask. Yes, there are many couples engaging in sexual intercourse because they feel this is what a married couple is must do. Many of them don't view it as a pleasurable and erotic activity. Instead of looking forward to those moments that are designed to be filled with ecstasy, they do it only out of a sense of obligation.

One cause could be connected to what I dealt with earlier in the section entitled "Spiritual Warfare." There are many couples who have witnessed some things in the past that could be affecting the present. Many have been wounded by some type of sexual abuse, which has caused them to literally hate the very thought of sex. The very act of sexual intercourse stirs up emotions from past encounters. And, instead of producing pleasure and happiness, it produces pain and hurt.

There are many who need to seek professional help in this area to cope with past events that continue to haunt them in their present relationship. For others, they simply need to witness freedom from the past by repenting of those past sexual encounters outside of the marital relationship. All you need to do in this instance is repent from your past sexual sins. If you are sincere, God will forgive you. Remember that 1 John 1:9 takes it a step further by saying, "If we confess our sins, He is faithful and just to forgive us our sins, and to *cleanse* us of all unrighteousness (emphasis added)" (KJV). Remember that since forgiveness and cleansing has taken place, you are free.

You don't have to worry about those past sins surfacing again. Hebrews 8:12 says, "For I will be merciful to their unrighteousness, and their sins and their iniquities will I remember no more" (KJV). Satan may try to use them against you, but remember that God has cleared the slate. When the writer of Hebrews speaks of God no longer remembering our past sins, he is not saying that God is no longer omniscient (all-knowing), he is simply reminding us that God will not bring those sins up anymore. Since God is not going to bring them up, why should we?

There are others who need to let go of the bitterness and grant forgiveness to those who abused them. This sounds like a hard thing to do. The truth is that it is going to be difficult due to the pain that you may have witnessed in the past. But remember, forgiveness provides you the opportunity to simply release the burden and turn it over to God. Satan has established a stronghold from which only God can deliver them. It is Satan's desire for you to remain miserable, but it is the desire of God for you to have "joy unspeakable."

I received permission to share a portion of a letter submitted to me a few years ago from a Christian woman who had been married for several years. She, along with hundreds of others, had an opportunity to attend a seminar in which Neil Anderson's "Steps to Freedom" were used to deliver people from their spiritual bondage. She writes:

Pastor Wesley, I am so glad that you had an opportunity to meet the author of the *Bondage Breaker*. I am even more excited that you decided to place your Bible study program on hold to concentrate on Mr. Anderson's material. The three months of emphasis placed on spiritual warfare that took place on Wednesday nights changed my life. After going through the "Seven Steps," I am now free. Let me share one area with you that has made a difference.

My husband ____ and I have a brand new relationship now. Sexual intercourse was more of a nightmare than a dream. I tried to find things to do late at night as an excuse not to go to bed when my husband did, so that we would not have sex. When I couldn't avoid it, I would make sure it was dark in the room so my husband wouldn't see the tears flowing. My husband thought he was the problem all these years. We had considered ending the marriage over this lack of sexual satisfaction. The problem wasn't my husband at all.

After going through the spiritual warfare series, I discovered that there was something buried in my past from childhood that caused the problems in my marriage. I was abused by a person that my parents trusted to take care of me. It only happened twice, but that was enough to ruin me for thirty years. After going through the steps to freedom, ____ and I enjoy lovemaking now. I actually tell him now to hurry to the bedroom. Thank God I am free!

There are many that can witness the restoration of pleasure in the bedroom by simply letting Satan know that they know the truth. Freedom is available to every husband and wife.

There is one more reason for the anti-pleasure state existing in some marriages, which I feel is connected to spiritual warfare (there are probably others). There may be some unresolved problems in the marriage. There are many marriages that have fallen victim to the "mean monster" along the way (see Section 4). The couple has decided to try to save the marriage, although one or the other has been an unfaithful partner. As you work on saving the marriage, lovemaking is extremely difficult, because you always find yourself thinking about the fact that he has been with another woman or she has been with another man.

Lovemaking has become a brick-wall experience. You go through the motions of having sex, but it lacks the pleasure that once existed. It takes time to deal with that period of unfaithfulness. However, it can work. It will take some time for the other partner to get past the unfaithfulness. But, if forgiveness has been truly granted, the restoration of pleasure will come. It is important for the unfaithful one to do what is necessary to pull the brick wall down. It is important for him or her to get rid of the "bulldozer" mentality in this process. Don't expect the brick wall to just come tumbling down. It will take some time. Even if it means pulling it down brick by brick.

It is Satan's desire for the faithful partner to hold the grudge and the anger against the unfaithful spouse. The devil will try to build on the lack of trust that now exists to drive the wedge even deeper than it already is. It will take a strong, praying couple to get through this period without letting Satan get the upper hand. The more time spent in prayer together, the quicker that wall will come down and the marriage will return to its rightful place. Remember that prayer and time are the keys to restoring the joy.

Another reason for the lack of pleasure is connected to what I call the "wham-bam-thank-you-ma'am" conduct of many men. There are many men who ignore Peter's advice when he says, "You husbands likewise, live with your wives in an understanding way . . ." (1 Pet. 3:7a KJV). There is a need for the husband to understand that his wife, although made of the same material as himself, is turned on differently than the way he is.

> I slept but my heart was awake. Listen! My lover is knocking: "Open to me, my sister, my darling, my dove, my flawless one. My head is drenched with dew, my hair with the dampness of the night." I have taken off my robe— must I put it on again? I have washed my feet— must I soil them again? My lover thrust his hand through the latch-opening; my heart began to pound for him. I arose to open for my lover, and my hands dripped with myrrh, my fingers with flowing myrrh, on the handles of the lock. I opened for my lover, but my lover had left; he was gone. My heart sank at his departure. I looked for him but did not find him. I called him but he did not answer. (Song of Solomon 5:2-6)

In Song of Solomon 5:2-6, note the flow of the romantic interlude. The passage suggests that there is a period of romancing and foreplay that takes place before intercourse occurs. I heard a very interesting analogy used to describe the difference between the husband and wife when it comes to sexual stimulation. The husband has a "microwave" sex drive, while the wife's is more like the "crockpot." One cooks slower than the other. Husbands should remember that sexual intercourse should be a time of pleasure for both. Therefore, stop breaking the speed limit!

Remember that God made it, therefore sex is a good thing. Since marriage is honorable and the bed undefiled, your bedroom should be considered one of the most sanctified rooms in the house. Since it is good and of God, you don't have to ask God out of the bedroom, either. He produced sexual intercourse for our pleasure. It is good. As a matter of fact, it is not sacrilegious for you to say, "Oh God, thanks," in the heat of the moment. All you are doing is thanking God for what He has blessed you with. Don't think that you are sinning. It is better for you to speak in those "unknown tongues" rather than some of the "known tongues" anyhow.

Centralizing the Scriptural Texts

God's Word is an awesome book. It addresses every subject that the devil desires to use against us. For example, there are too many couples who are using their bodies as weapons. The wife who is angry with her husband says, "I'll show him tonight when he wants what he won't get." Or, there is the husband who has been full of energy all month, and when he knows that this is the time of the month his wife needs him most when it comes to sexual intercourse, he turns over and says, "I had a hard day and I am too tired." Listen to what the Bible says about this subject of depriving one another:

> Let the husband fulfill his duty to his wife, and likewise also the wife to her husband. The wife does not have authority over her own body, but the husband does; and likewise the husband does not have authority over his own body, but the wife does. Stop depriving one another,

except by agreement for a time that you may devote yourselves to prayer, and come together again lest Satan tempt
you because of your lack of self-control. (1 Cor. 7:3–5
KJV)

I love this "equal rights" section of the Scripture dealing with the duties assigned to the husband and wife regarding sex. It is our God-given duty to engage in sexual
activity when the other spouse desires to. It is sinful for the
husband or wife to deprive the other from having that sexual
moment with him or her. If he wants to, you must oblige
him. If she wants to, you must oblige her. He has been given
the rights over his wife's body. She has been given the rights
over her husband's body. There is an exception clause noted
in those verses. The couple can agree on an abstinence period for prayer purposes only. This time of prayer is permit-
ted but must not be prolonged for spiritual safety reasons.

The devil would love for the couple to have problems
in this area. He realizes that he can use the "spousal re-
fusal" as ammunition to work. Satan will allow more temptations to surface to try to lure the spouse wanting sex.
There are many couples who have fallen into his trap. There
is no justifiable reason for extramarital affairs. But Satan
does not live by that rule. His rule says: "If he or she won't
feed you at home, go out to eat!" You should satisfy your
spouse's sexual needs.

There is a word of caution I must interject here. Sexual
intercourse should always be a time of pleasure as mentioned earlier. When a person tries to take what is not freely
given, he can possibly have his needs met, but what about
your covenant partner? There are too many men who fail
to give their wives the time of day and then expect sexual
satisfaction. This is not what God had in mind.

Remember that God expects us to do as He has instructed us throughout the Scripture. Don't just select verses to support your wishes and whims. I know one brother who can quote these verses of Scripture verbatim. He will tell his wife that she must have sex according to 1 Corinthians 7. I want to say to that husband that he is accurate, but he must learn some other verses, such as the one that says, "Husbands love your wives, even as Christ also loved the church . . ." (Eph. 5:25 KJV).

If your mate becomes sexually stimulated, you should "render due benevolence." Give him or her what is needed to satisfy. The Bible commands you to. I had a wife attending a marriage seminar to question this point once by asking, "What if one or the other is physically unable to make love because of the flu or something?" I shared that this is a good time to agree on a period of prayer. If you just can't perform, you just can't do it. When you live in understanding of one another, this really will not be a problem. But if you always have a headache or something, there is a serious problem with you denying your spouse.

Another question that surfaced from a husband attending a seminar was, "What about when your spouse is snoring the moment she gets in the bed?" This is probably the most common one of them all. Let's face it, when you have worked ten hours, rushed home to prepare a meal, helped the kids with the homework, made sure all of them had their baths, and pulled out all of the clothes for another day, you can understand why one falls asleep fast. The first thing to accept is that her fatigue is just as legitimate as your sexual desire. The pillow becomes a cloud traveling to dreamland after the body has done so much.

After accepting the fact that the fatigue is legitimate due to the various tasks, evaluate the causes of the fatigue to see if you can help ease the load. There are times when we can share certain responsibilities that will cause us to have an energy reserve that can be used for other pleasurable things. Periodically, plan on taking the family out for dinner so that the hours spent preparing a meal are cut out. Or get with your child's teacher and see if you can receive the study plans and assignments early, in order help your kids with the homework in advance.

Another thing to consider is that sometimes, sexual stimulation caused before you stretched out in the bed can sometimes overpower the fatigue. In other words, you would be surprised at what could happen as you help her to get undressed to take her evening bath. Or, you may be surprised to see what results from washing her back and massaging her body as she soaks in the tub. The fatigue will not disappear, but in most cases it will move over to allow sexual stimulation to occur.

Plain ordinary tiredness is probably the most common single problem working against a successive sexual relationship. That's why sexual play and intercourse are often far better at some time other than bedtime, when one or both of you are just "too tired." Your waterbed should never become the Dead Sea.

Cementing the Stimulating Treats

What can couples do to keep the sex drive out of neutral? It is important for couples to analyze their relationship and implement special steps to cement special times of pleasure. Listed below are some simple suggestions that comprise what I like to call the "Sex Scene Survival Kit":

1. *Avoid the I Love Lucy set up.*

I love watching the old reruns of *I Love Lucy*. The problem that always concerned me was the sleeping arrangements. They slept in twin beds. At first, I thought this was due to them not having enough money for one Queen-size bed, until I saw the episode of them buying new furniture. They replaced the old twin beds with new twin beds. If you want sexual intimacy to remain, sleep together.

2. *If you dress to tease, you may get undressed to please.*

There is nothing wrong with a Christian husband or a Christian wife dressing to turn each other on. If you only wear the old cotton pajamas, don't get mad if she fails to be tempted. If the gown you wear resembles something from the eighteenth century, don't get mad if he does not become excited. Your spouse needs both visual stimulation as well as physical stimulation.

3. *Turn off the light, but light a candle.*

Total darkness is not wise when it comes to making love. You want your spouse making love to you, not lying in bed trying to remember what you look like. I believe that all five senses are at work with lovemaking.

4. *Turn off the television.*

You don't need any distractions. It is hard for one to be stimulated while certain things are going on. There isn't anything that great on the tube anyhow at certain hours. It is a rerun of Perry Mason that will be shown next week at some time.

5. *Foreplay is like the warm-up before the game.*

Find out what she likes before sex. Find those erroneous zones requiring that special touch. There is nothing wrong with asking him what he likes before you actually engage in sex.

6. *Produce names and signs to voice your desires with your spouse.*

There is nothing wrong with your use of code language about sexual desires. Let him know that your "thermostat" is on. Let her know that her "buddy" is up and calling for her. It is OK, because remember, what is yours is his and vice versa.

7. *Take advantage of those children's nights out.*

I tell couples at the church often to take advantage of those two-hour youth functions at the church. I tell them to sometimes leave their children for certain youth functions at church and go home and have a ball. I tell them just to make sure they don't fall asleep afterwards. Come back and pick up your children.

8. *Express the pleasure you witnessed doing, and after, the moments of ecstasy.*

Tell her or tell him how you felt when this or that was done. As a matter of fact, while it is going on, tell him not to stop. Tell her to stay right there.

9. *Don't allow the bedroom to be the only lovemaking station in your house.*

If the fire of desire starts burning while in front of the fireplace, go for it! The bed is only the best for some because they haven't tried it anywhere else.

Remember that sex was specifically produced by God for married couples only. God intended for it to be a time of pleasure and not pain. Satan will try to prevent us from witnessing the pleasure of the moment. Since sex was produced by God, it is something good when operating within the perimeters of biblical principles. Husbands and wives should be willing to fulfill each other's sexual needs.

Conclusion

In concluding this book on marriage, let me comment on some additional areas that you may find beneficial. I believe the implementation of the things discussed in this book will help to pull the marriage out of the pit of hell. It is important for you to do all that you can to keep it on a heavenly plane. A good way to keep the marriage there is to establish a covenant with your spouse. This covenant, or agreement, will help keep the marriage in check. This agreement is not designed to replace the Word of God. As a matter of fact, the agreement should be supported by the Scripture. It should serve as a reminder of what God has already revealed through His Word.

The agreement should be as concise and comprehensive as possible. Let's look at an example of one of those agreements.

If This Marriage Was Made In Heaven,
Why Am I Going Through Hell?

Our Covenant Commitment Charge:

Challenge
I will challenge my covenant partner to do his/her best in all projects.

Compliment
I will compliment my covenant partner frequently.

Consult
I will consult my covenant partner concerning issues that effect our partnership.

Coordinate
I will coordinate my schedule to provide as much quality family time as possible.

Call
I will show common courtesy by calling when my scheduled time of arrival has the possibility of changing drastically.

Communicate
I will communicate my concerns with my covenant partner without making him/her guess what is wrong.

Create
I will create "special" moments to keep the fire burning in the marriage.

Consideration
I will consider my spouse's feelings at all times before I act or react.

Concentrate
I will concentrate on my covenant partner's needs, so that I can do my part in fulfilling them.

Commitment
I will commit to all of these agreements and whatever else it takes to make this the greatest marriage ever.

The Anniversary Check-Up

There are special things we do for our bodies and vehicles that we should incorporate in our marriages. There are times when we go and have our annual physicals taken to see if we are healthy or not. We do this because we realize there are some illnesses that may not be visible from the surface. The problem can exist before the pain comes. If there is a problem that is not visible to the human eye, it is possible that the technological equipment will detect it in time.

Also, we allow our vehicles to go in to the shop for service. We don't wait until we have transmission trouble before we go. We don't wait until we blow a gasket or engine before we go. We try to prevent these things from happening by going in for our 20,000-mile service. We try to prevent this by getting an oil and lube job done frequently.

Our marriages deserve the same attention. We should take advantage of attending special seminars on marriage. We should enroll in special marriage enrichment programs and classes at our local churches, even when there is nothing seriously wrong in the marriage. Maybe you can schedule an annual check-up with the pastor of counseling around your anniversary time. Remember the old cliché that says, "A stitch in time saves nine."

In conclusion, the institution of marriage can only work when we allow the Scripture to exist in our lives. We can rebuild what the devil has attempted to destroy. In the process of rebuilding, we must carefully choose what material we will use.

I love the story of the "Three Little Pigs." The big, bad wolf was out to destroy life for the three little pigs. All of the pigs had shelter. One of the pigs had a shelter made out of the right stuff. When the wolf decided to "huff and puff and try to blow the third house down," he couldn't because the house was made out of rock.

If we want our rocky marriages to not only survive but thrive, we need to place that rocky marriage on the Rock. We need Jesus, the Rock of our salvation, to serve as the solid foundation for our marriages. When the devil tries to blow the marriage down, he will fail. We will see our marriages getting stronger and stronger.

We allow the devil to put us through so much unnecessary agony simply because we don't spend enough time in the Word of God. As a couple, spend some time studying the passages of Scripture about marriage. But remember that you can't just apply the passages of Scripture dealing with marriage only. You must apply the Word of God to your life.

To order additional copies of

If This Marriage
Was Made In Heaven,
Why Am I Going
Through Hell?

Call (877) 421-READ

or send $12.99 each plus $3.95* S&H

WinePress Publishing
P.O. Box 428
Enumclaw, WA 98022
*add $1.00 for each additional book ordered

or

Antioch Fellowship Baptist Church
7408 S Hampton Rd.
Dallas, Texas 75232
(972) 228-2420